Finding Your Edge: Establishing and Maintaining Boundaries When You Work From Home

Maya Middlemiss

ISBN: 979-871-6-81-7418

TABLE OF CONTENTS:

FOREWORD

We all have limits as human beings. No-one of us has endless energy, resources, time, resilience or strength. Establishing and maintaining our boundaries, helps us keep and KNOW our edges. Exploring and finding our limits, in our key areas of life not only serves a purpose of knowing our own individual limits. It also defines the scope of any particular area and also helps us frame how those "borders" work together. There can be tension, of course. However, I find if I look from one part of my life (when I undertake a hobby) and look back over to another part (to my professional work). I get perspective.

With no limits, we may find that the colours all bleed into one another and our priorities and focus may be confused. How do we find that overall understanding, scope (to say no) and then gain perspective? Only by taking the time needed to understand how these all work together.

The second part of the Healthy Happy Homeworking Series by Maya Middlemiss, Finding Your Edge, is a comprehensive and accessible review of all the things you need to consider in your individual approach to setting up your home office. Moving through all the relevant considerations; from technology through to our senses and how we comprehend our work tasks. Reviewing each of these parts, helps us understand the full view, gain awareness in how the jigsaw fits together and how by examining the perimeter of each part, we really can gain an "edge" in our work-life-integration and effectiveness as a home worker.

Forward by Rowena Hennigan, Remote Work Expert, Lecturer, Course Author & Consultant

CHAPTER 1: INTRODUCTION

Boundaries and why we need them

According to dictionary.com, a boundary is defined as "a line which marks the limits of an area; a dividing line".

While I am not sure, when it comes to work, that there is always a visible line to be inspected - which is a big part of the problem - this particular working definition serves fairly well. A boundary, then, is a divider of some kind, one state of things being, compared with an alteration which happens on the other side of it.

When you're working in a traditional office, you step into a designated building to do it. Within that building there may be other physical boundaries you also naturally embrace: that's the meeting room, this is my desk/office, that area is for hot-desking, or storage, or social breaks, and so on. There may even be explicit signage clarifying the purpose of different rooms, so no one is in any doubt of the shared meanings and understandings.

There is also the big boundary at the edge of all the others, separating the workplace from everything else in your life - although arguably, for knowledge workers of all descriptions, technology has been eroding this boundary steadily for years. The last time I had to take a morning train into London, I don't think I saw a single person simply relaxing with a newspaper or a book. So, boundaries are more than physical spaces, even if that's one of the first things you might consider should you find yourself needing to work from home unexpectedly.

Most of us operating within the sphere of knowledge work of any description must obtain clarity regarding the boundaries of the work itself. Unlike stamping out a target number of widgets on a production line, there may not be any hard edges to indicate 'done' (enough) for the day. Often then, we rely on cues to indicate the acceptable boundaries, such as 'Done all I can by around 6 when everyone else leaves,' although these unwritten rules are vulnerable to attrition by expectation, hustle culture, and presenteeism. We might have leaky boundaries on our personal technology too, especially if our work email or messaging app is installed on our mobile phone. It's not easy to draw those lines and step away.

So we all need to pay attention to our boundaries, and for the homeworker, there are special issues around the lines - or otherwise - between personal and domestic space in particular, and also the time, attention and consumption that these potentially conflicting priorities can generate.

In volume 2 of the *Healthy Happy Homeworking* series, I invite you to consider how these visible or invisible boundaries impact on you and your work and everyone around you, and consider how you can establish and enforce them where necessary. You might need to make big changes in your environment, in order to ensure your wellbeing and effectiveness at work. Or you may find you can make some small, subtle tweaks which have a big impact and really help you protect the 'Not Work' aspect of your life from the ever-growing tendency of work to spread and take over.

Martyrdom is the selfish approach

Before we dive in, however, I just want to make one essential thing clear. From my personal experience, and also from my reader research, I know that some people need to first understand the most important thing: **Boundaries are necessary, vital, and responsible. They are not selfish.**

On the other hand, to allow yourself to be walked on, steamrollered, overwhelmed, overruled, and burned out is bad for everything, and everyone, in your life.

There's a reason the safety card requires you to fasten your own oxygen mask first before assisting others, and that is that those others are depending on you to be there for them - whether they're colleagues, clients, family, or friends. If you don't draw up your edges and defend them, defend yourself, and protect your boundaries, then you will end up letting others down at some point. There's really nothing heroic about taking on more and more until you fall apart, just as there's nothing weak or lazy about saying 'Enough already! I am at my limit/this is not my job/ I am not taking on additional responsibilities/ I have to do X as a priority right now then I will get back to you', or a million other variations on the same theme.

Similarly, you absolutely must make time for self-care, for exercise, for eating well, and so on. If others depend on you, you will let them down in far bigger ways when you fail to do this, and you'll burn out if you don't protect your boundaries.

Here's the really short version, for you to practice in front of the mirror until you're confident. Learn to say "No!" As Annie Lamott observed, 'No' is a complete sentence.

If the very idea of saying 'No!' makes you squirm, please read on.

You have already taken the first step, because you've actually got this book about defining and defending your boundaries, in your hands right now. Whatever way others may have come to perceive you, you are *not* a doormat. You have limits, and you have a right to those boundaries. Other people might have very valid expectations of you to behave in a certain way, as a colleague or a parent or a partner or whatever, and that's absolutely fine. But those expectations need their parameters to be defined and made explicit. Often people will thank you for that, and at the very least, they'll respect your self-awareness and your limits.

Within teams and groups, when you are clear and assertive about your boundaries, it actually makes it easier for other people to reciprocate and state their own, so you really can set in motion a positive feedback loop where everyone understands and allows for each other a bit more.

I don't just mean at work, - this is equally applicable within your family, or your babysitting circle, or your parents' WhatsApp group-

So if you are one of the people who needs to read this bit before moving on, I hope you can now at least glimpse the possibility of how things could be different, if you get a grip on your boundaries. The rest of this book - and indeed the other titles in the *Healthy Happy Homeworking* series, to varying extents - will equip you with the tools and tactics to make it so.

But they are *your* boundaries - and only you can define, establish, and maintain them.

CHAPTER 2: PHYSICAL SPACE AND BOUNDARIES

When you're not rocking up daily to a big building with a sign saying 'The Office,' one of your biggest spatial boundary definers is gone.

Also gone is a space which was probably built and designed specifically for its purpose, with very different qualities to a domestic space, in terms of decor, acoustics, access, lighting, furnishing, technology, and so on. You probably wouldn't want to live in an office, so what happens when you find yourself losing all that makes that space what it is, and having to work in your living zone instead?

Naturally enough, your first inclination is to recreate that familiar work environment at home, and in many ways that makes a lot of sense. But pause for one moment first, because there are things to consider from a long way back.

The first is that you may have new constraints. In fact, you almost certainly do - there will be things you used to in a traditional office building that you cannot easily recreate at home, whatever your resources, from the IT support team down the hall to the conference room you used once a month. You'll have to find ways of making space and resources work for you in new ways, and that requires new thinking.

The second aspect to setting up your workspace, which is easy to overlook, is that you have new opportunities now.

You're not stuck with the standard suppliers, lighting, colour schemes, and so on. While you might have a budget or resources from your employer which dictate certain things, it's your home and your space, so you should be able to negotiate considerably more discretion. Without spending lots of money, it's perfectly possible to carve out space to work in that feels like home, rather than thinking you have to exactly replicate the office within your house.

This is a tiny example, but why would you choose a plastic Ikea or Staples litter bin? Why not chuck your biscuit wrappers in something prettier, which looks like it belongs in a home, rather than an office? Similarly, why not disguise your cabling and chargers behind some attractive plants or upholstery, so your tech looks like it belongs in a living room rather than a server room? Pick out some artwork that inspires you, whether it's a favourite print, or something your kids created with love, and hang it where you can see it, rather than only thinking about what shows up on your webcam.

Your aesthetic choices are your own, so don't underestimate their impact on your mood, and don't think that working from home means creating the office in your home. I believe small personal touches like choosing luxury stationery and desk accessories means they more than earn their keep if they make you feel good while you work. So keep that in mind, as you reflect upon the physical boundaries of your home office.

A room of your own

For many people forced to work from home unexpectedly, the lack of a dedicated area, never mind room, can be the greatest challenge. Having for years enjoyed the luxury of my own comfortable and private home office, it's difficult to imagine what everyone was up against in 2020, when they were suddenly told they had to work from home overnight. Here in Spain, where apartment living is the norm within cities, many families don't really have dining rooms or second reception rooms, and guest rooms are a luxury. It isn't even a class thing here, since a lot of wealthy urban households are geared up for a highly social lifestyle involving rarely eating at home, and they were hugely impacted by these lockdown changes. Never mind the unthinkable impact on families living in already cramped and less than ideal accommodation, and fighting to share small devices for work and study purposes.

It's the same in cities across the world, where younger professionals in particular often choose their accommodation based on location and access to facilities (including work/commuting), rather than for spaciousness. An urban flat-share with people you don't even know that well might work fine when you're all up and out of the door all day every day. However, I know a lot of people who had more time than they ever wanted to get to know all their flatmates' most intimate quirks during lockdown, quite apart from having to negotiate time at the kitchen table to actually be productive.

So, finding space to work can be a nightmare, and I'd encourage you to think about what you need from your workspace as a basic principle, then go from there to see how best to meet those needs, based on the resources you have to hand.

Yes, in an ideal world that would probably be a dedicated room you use as an office every day, then close the door on at night, to be used for no other purpose and by no other person. If working from home is a long-term lifestyle choice for you, then I encourage you to aspire to this setup, even if it means making sacrifices in other areas. It's like those adverts you see about investing in a really good mattress because you spend a third of your life in bed or something. Surely the proportion of time you spend in full-time work is just as great, and deserves similar prioritising, when you next make a decision about where to live.

I would argue, for the same reason, that it shouldn't default to being the tiniest, pokiest room in the house either, so there is at the very least a conversation to be had about that. I was talking to a friend in real estate recently who is already seeing demand shooting up for that extra bedroom, reception, or terrace that people previously managed without. I am sure we'll see much bigger changes in how we use physical space at the urban planning level, with people migrating to suburbs and smaller community hubs, and urban business districts undergoing a true transformation.

That's a different book though. For now, you need to work with where you are today, and take a long, hard look at what you need - and how best to meet that need with the resources you have available to you.

It's a bit like when you're dieting to lose weight, and you're really craving a crunchy chocolate bar. A diet counsellor might suggest you reflect first on what need that's really going to fulfil, in order to make you pause and examine the craving. So if you're feeling that your stomach is empty, drink a glass of water, or if it's the snap and the crunch you miss, then eating a stick of celery might do the trick...

No, that doesn't work for me either, just give me the damn chocolate! However, when it comes to thinking about work space, you might be able to use this mind game more effectively.

For example, if you really need an ergonomic desk and chair *right now*, perhaps you can repurpose a table or a worktop at home, so you only need to buy or borrow the chair part, if you can get one which is height adjustable?

Is there a gamer lurking in a bedroom somewhere, with a very comfortable desk-level chair you can co-opt for the duration, if you need to work from home temporarily? I am sure they wouldn't mind. And if all I said about standing desks and desk risers in volume one remains out of reach right now, perhaps there are other surfaces in your home, like a shelf or a kitchen worktop you could use from time to time instead, for standing up work.

If your space is not ideal for working from home, it's going to mean improvisation of one kind or another, but you could consider a tip from a recent office accommodation trend - the future of which now seems uncertain - hot-desking.

Hot-desking in the workplace usually involves not having a dedicated workspace, and either working from somewhere different each day, or sharing a desk on a timed basis with a particular partner or small group of colleagues. They recently introduced hot-desking at our main bank branch, and what this now involves is your advisor meeting you in the lobby, then trotting around anxiously trying to find a meeting room or space, depending on the privacy or urgency constraints of your appointment. It certainly doesn't feel ideal for meeting clients, nor does this institution seem to have embraced the paperless and cloud-based approach for which it is best suited, as the advisors are continually lugging around piles of documents and files clutched to their laptops, as they scour for a spot they are apparently unable to pre-book.

But at home, you can make better arrangements. If you and a partner are temporarily forced to work from home, perhaps you can reduce your 'office' down to its absolute bare essentials, like a laptop and a notebook, and timeshare the available space.

Then it's easy to tidy away at the end of your shift, so your partner can work in the space, and vice versa. Making this work means a commitment to the tidying and resetting each day, out of respect for the other person - but if it means you both get a few hours in the quiet room rather than the home-schooling room, then it's worth a shot.

A lot of this will be a case of trial and error when circumstances are not ideal, and it's worth being creative and open minded. Here are some suggestions to consider, from around the Healthy Happy Homeworking community online:

"I don't have room for a separate office, but I bought a room divider screen cheaply online - in fact I got it to use as a background for video calls, to hide the messy living room, but found I use it when I log off at night to screen off that corner of the room and make a physical boundary between work and my own time. Then I don't have to pack all my work stuff away every time, which helps me get going in the morning, but I don't have to look at it over dinner either."

"In our apartment we have basically one spot that works for doing webcam meetings, without it being obvious we're in a kitchen or bedroom. So my flatmate and I work around sharing that, and we need to be aware of each other's meeting schedules."

"I work in various parts of the apartment, but I will not work in my bedroom. For some reason I just have to GO to work, even if that means stepping into the kitchen. I don't have a spare room but will work from anywhere if I have to, just not the place I sleep and do all my other favourite things."

"Working from home has enabled me to personalise my space, even though it's the tiniest room you couldn't even fit an adult bed in. It may even be smaller than my cubicle was in the office, but I have cheerful art on the walls, and flowers, and my aromatherapy diffuser. It actually feels more like my zone of the house, than anywhere else does!"

So many creative ideas emerge from the solving of problems related to space usage. You can also take inspiration from the 'Tiny Homes' movement, and some amazing architectural solutions, or from a friend of Rowena's who folds her workstation into a wheeled cart every evening so she can easily stow it out of sight in a cupboard.

Recreating or repurposing space

While some people - like the clients of my real estate friend above - might be in a position to move house in order to accommodate home working, most of us aren't going to be able to do that overnight. So if you are trying to carve out a dedicated office in a home you never chose with that in mind, here are some ideas to consider:

The guest room

Having whole rooms dedicated to people who might at some point come to visit can feel like a luxury, particularly these days, and often with a bit of thought a spare bedroom can become a multi-purpose space instead. With the help of a sofa bed, and a desk and storage space that is more domestic in appearance than utilitarian, you can easily create a room which converts, when needed, into a space for visitors.

Make sure you can tidy away sensitive or messy work items, and have a Plan B for any extended visits (like taking your laptop back to the kitchen table for a bit if you have to). Also, don't get lazy about working on the sofa bed! See volume 1 for discussion of the ergonomics of sofa working, but the short version is, it's very bad for your back and neck.

Nooks and crannies

I have seen some amazingly creative home offices carved out of the tiniest physical spaces, yet still managing to create their own physical boundaries and a bit of dedicated 'office'. A gorgeous old-fashioned roll-top desk makes an attractive piece of living room furniture, while concealing a multitude of messy work-related sins if you actually close it up at night. I saw an Ikea corner desk in a hallway someone had built wooden doors across - which she opened for work during her office hours, then closed firmly in the evenings.

Even under the stairs can work as office space. Not necessarily behind cupboard doors Harry Potter style, but if you take the doors off altogether and find somewhere else to stash the hoover and the Christmas decorations, there might be quite a lot of space lurking there, which can accommodate a desk and shelves without intruding too much on domestic life.

The garden office

Do you have space outside to accommodate an outbuilding of some description? Many purpose-built home office units are small in footprint and designed to fit carefully within requirements for planning consents. They are also quick to install from prefabricated parts, without requiring much in the way of access, and causing minimal disruption.

If you're self-employed, then this is naturally a business expense (and it also helps avoid potential confusion regarding the official use of your main home and any capital gain it might make). If you're employed, you can make an excellent case to your employer as to the benefits of having a distinct office with clear boundaries away from domestic disturbances. In either case, financing might well be available, either from the unit manufacturer or the usual business credit sources. Once it's paid for, it adds value to your home, as future occupants could use it for various non-office purposes, and some units can even be taken with you and reassembled elsewhere.

From personal experience, this can be a great solution, but you will need to pay attention to many aspects of comfort, just as you would with any room you were going to sit in for hours every day, all year round. You cannot realistically work in a garden shed, you need light and insulation and so on, installed to a specification designed for spending prolonged time within. You will need heating in the winter, and fans or aircon in the summer, and of course you need cabling for electricity (and broadband, though you may be able to reach your home router with some judiciously spaced repeaters). If you're going to leave your work stuff there overnight, which is really the whole idea when it comes to boundaries, you will need to think about security too. Conventional home contents insurance may specifically exclude such outbuildings from cover, and the doors and lock supplied with it may be inadequate if you have your own small Apple Store franchise at the end of the garden path.

I once had a unit like this in my garden which accommodated me and several colleagues, but it was complicated and more expensive than I had anticipated, and there were interesting unexpected fun moments. Like running down there in the middle of the night because a spider had crawled across the burglar alarm sensor, for example. I would probably have preferred to encounter armed robbers at that moment, but usually it was fine, and it made sense as a property improvement long term.

Working from home, or living at work?

While most people end up working in one particular space or location, part of the joy of working from home is that you can be a lot more flexible, and indeed I urge you to think about the space you have around you more creatively than you might be able to in somebody else's building.

Perhaps there are different parts of your working day, or different activities, which lend themselves to different locations? Reading and research can be done just as well from a sofa, standing meetings at a bookcase or a kitchen counter, to switch up the energy and vary your working day.

A word of caution on the boundaries front though. While this can work very well, particularly for highly integrated homeworkers (see 'task and work boundaries', below), you might want to keep a few hard edges here.

I go out of my way in these books and my client work to consider different needs and avoid being prescriptive, and I often find myself in a quirky blend of irritated and amused by the various 'Rules for working from home' articles you find, which are frequently written by columnists who never do so regularly. I believe that when it's your home, no real rules apply other than your own.

I do encourage you to think through *your* rules though, and at the very least have a couple of red lines you will not cross, where work cannot be permitted into your personal life, time, and space.

The Rules type listicles will say 'Never work from your bed' - which you might want to consider. Perhaps you have to work from your bed though, because you're sick and you're on a deadline, or your central heating is broken and it's the warmest spot. Perhaps instead there's one favourite armchair where you love to read magazines and watch TV, and instead THAT is the boundary you will impose, and you'd rather sit on the floor than ever work from that spot. This is really important, so protect that space, ensuring that it will always signify home/not-work whenever you sink gracefully into its familiar upholstery.

Or you may have a favourite view out of the window which common sense might suggest is a good location for your desk, but actually, this aspect is so personal and relaxing to you that you'd prefer to turn your desk to the wall and save that vista for non-work appreciation.

There have to be edges, where the workplace stops and the home begins.

The Rules also say never work in pyjamas, or even wear full-on business dress to 'go to work' from home. This one has never worked for me in any way. I regard clothing as highly functional, and the function of clothes for working from home is to be comfortable and appropriate to the ambient temperature, plus whatever else I might be doing that day. This could mean a slightly smart top if I have an important call, or it might mean swimwear or yoga pants or whatever other healthy thing I think I might be more inclined to do later on. It might even mean both.

For me, it will never involve a suit or anything similar, but if it helps you to go to work in formal wear, then go for it. Just like you might be more confident in that online meeting if you wear full makeup, or a perfume that no video-conferencing platform can yet convey the effect of, even if you download the latest version, if helps YOU feel more confident or professional or beautiful, then have at it. Wear a ballgown or fancy dress, or yes, even your PJs if they are comfortable the rest of the time, because it's YOUR home, your work, your mood, your boundaries, and that's all that matters. You can always pretend you left a filter on Zoom by mistake, if you accidently show up to a work meeting in your Monsters Inc onesie.

Alternatively, change into your PJs to signal to yourself that the work is at an end and the day is done, if that helps.

Here are some ideas for creating boundary conditions. They won't always make it into an odd-numbered clickbait listicle of 'rules' on popular websites, but you might want to think about instigating the following:

- No TV or radio on in 'the office'/during office hours, in shared areas. Anything which creates distraction will just make the working day longer and less productive anyway.

- No eating at your desk - take a proper break for meals, even if it's a few feet away. I observe this one as strictly as I can, but obviously coffee is an exception and can be mainlined at any time.

- Stay off work-related messaging and social media during the evenings at home (or at the very least, during mealtimes).

- No work apps on the front page of the home screen of your phone (see tech and boundaries, below).

- No removal of chargers, cables, post-it notes, highlighters, or ANY OF MY STUFF from my desk, at any time. Not even when you're just borrowing it and I wasn't there to ask and you really need it right now and anyway... *"You weren't even using it Mum!"* Anyone with teenagers in the house, can you relate to this?

CHAPTER 3: SENSORY BOUNDARIES

Whatever the physical logistics of your home size, you can explore the impact of different sensory input on the work you do, and experiment with what you can switch up to make things better.

Sounds like the office

One reason a lot of people like working from home is the peace and quiet it brings them, away from the bustle, interruption and noise that continually surrounds us all. Indeed, the shared open-plan offices which are - or were - very fashionable in many businesses can have very high levels of background hum, long before anyone pops over for a quick chat with you. This is one reason I prefer homeworking to anything like a co-working space or café, incidentally. I love a bit of peace.

Not everybody does though, so if you are working from home and find it too quiet, the good news is that you ARE at home - so you can have the background noise you choose. Sometimes you can't create a physical boundary, but you can carve out an auditory one. This might be essential for your concentration anyway, or for making and receiving business calls, but there's more to this issue than simply getting everyone around you to stop making such a bloody racket…

You can use music, or even other noises, to create psychological boundaries and cues to help you establish where work begins or ends.

This works for a friend I spoke to, simply by 'Blasting Radiohead at high volume until all teenagers have buggered off out of the dining room,' but your mileage will vary, and it's absolutely a matter of preference and taste. Personally, I usually prefer to write in silence, but I have been known to put on some familiar tunes if the mood takes me. I generally find instrumental, classical or modern classical music best of all, because otherwise I too easily find myself listening to the lyrics, instead of finding my own words. If you're not sure what to listen to for your productivity and pleasure it's well worth experimenting, and Spotify and similar services have their own suggestions of playlists curated for concentration, study, writing, focusing, or whatever best resonates with you.

Music can help drown out other noise too, although as a rule adding to the volume in that way can be bad for your ears as well as your concentration, even if it is Radiohead.

For those who find silence deafening, Spotify has created a standalone website called https://soundofcolleagues.com/ which lets you either livestream a continual cacophony of other people's chatter, coffee machines printer noises, and desktop alerts, or select specialised playlists like 'Corporate Office in the Middle of a City" or "Start-up Office Friday Afternoon" (the mind boggles).

Insane gimmick or a wonderful idea? Let me know what you think. I'll be at home, hiding under my desk, and wearing earplugs for good measure. It sounds like my idea of sheer hell or the worst co-working ever, but the attention it's attracting certainly suggests there's a nostalgic demand, during forced homeworking times at least, for that background buzz of other people doing stuff. And there's a definite case for having some kind of non-distracting white noise in the background to help filter concentration in various situations. Spotify also has playlists for things like rain on windowpanes or babbling brooks and so on, if that's more your preference.

And consider Brain FM, which claims to help you focus (or relax, depending on the track), by providing specific kinds of sounds for neuronal entrainment. I have experimented with this and I find it works quite well in terms of helping me concentrate, but whether that's due to the trance-like sounds (there's a choice) or something specifically impacting my brainwaves I'd hesitate to say. I am a control sample of one person here, though the research on their site is interesting to dig in to.

For me, I find it of value in a boundary sense though, and I like to use it when I am switching to a new piece of work or into a new context.

Ideally, you will use these kinds of sounds to provide texture to your home workplace when it's unfamiliarly quiet. For general noise control, (and the health of your eardrums) it's better to control sound by blocking out what you don't want, rather than drowning one sound with another.

If a closed door or even a curtain is not available, noise-cancelling headphones can be an asset. Even if you're not listening to anything, just putting them on can cocoon you in silence from the rest of the household, or from the traffic outside. Indeed, there's a tradition of developers using these in tech start-ups to create concentration space in busy offices, before everyone realised they could simply work from home instead. This could be an agreed signal in a shared home office, that headphones mean 'do not disturb,' in which case you will want to make sure they're comfortable for long hours of use.

Any headphones generally need to fit correctly over your ears to work properly, and not everyone likes them. Personally, I find the effect claustrophobic, and the racket would have to be pretty intrusive for the cost benefit to be worthwhile, but I have never taken the trouble to get accustomed to them, in fairness. The new Apple ones are certainly tempting and probably light as a feather, but not on the wallet, so I have resisted temptation so far.

If you think this will help you create a valued boundary between your work and the rest of your life in a noisy or distracting environment, then get the best headphones you can afford, to provide maximum noise control and comfort. You probably won't be surprised to learn that the more expensive ones are better, and often this means being physically lighter and smaller, as well as offering higher quality audio. And while electronic noise-cancelling will never be quite as effective as physically blocking the sound with huge cams, high-end in-ear devices like AirPods do a fairly impressive job of keeping ambient sounds out of your Zoom call or similar.

When choosing headphones, do remember that a Bluetooth or DECT connection, while also adding cost, will give you more freedom and flexibility for those ergonomic moves and stretches, and also won't make you feel like you are physically wired to your laptop. That's why I like my little AirPods. However, one issue sometimes reported with Bluetooth is interference, so if you are sharing space with lots of other people working from home or even sharing a building, many different things can introduce crackle, even a microwave oven!

The other thing about Bluetooth or otherwise cordless peripherals is they have a tendency to run out of battery at a critical moment, so at the very least a cheap USB headset is handy to have stashed in a drawer as a Plan B backup when your manager wants to jump on a call unexpectedly.

In further praise of inexpensive USB headsets, a reader of *Out of the Office* shared this anecdote with me about his experiences during lockdown homeworking:

"With three teenagers studying and two adults working, I'd been most worried about the broadband holding up - but actually that was fine. Instead, the noise levels generated were unbearable, just trying to find places for us all to be on calls or listening to things at the same time in different corners of the house was a nightmare. The school had said working from their bedrooms was to be discouraged, so we were all trying to find corners of the living room and kitchen where we could concentrate and hear ourselves think to work or study.

"After taking a call from my boss while sitting on the stairs one afternoon, I had to do something… So, I ordered 5 basic USB headsets with mics, from that online store we're so dependent on. They were less than €10 each, and they arrived the next day… What a life-changing miracle!

"Now everyone can sit around the table together, working side-by-side, with next to zero racket. None of that horrible feedback whine, or the boys turning up their speakers like their teachers are in some kind of rap battle, which reaches migraine level well before lunchtime.

"My only regret is getting 5 identical ones, so everyone could argue endlessly about whose was which, but you can't get everything right!"

Another reader reminded me that it's not just other people within your home who create noise, which can impact on your ability work:

"Frankly it took some negotiating with my neighbours when we started working from home, as they're students and don't exactly keep office hours.

29

We've ended up agreeing they can have their music on pretty late, so long as we can work in peace for most of the day. It's not ideal, but this time has been all about compromising - and it's not their fault the sound insulation is so bad in our building."

That's a more tolerant attitude than I often feel toward neighbours who suddenly feel a desperate urge to use chainsaws or pneumatic drills (at least that's what it sounds like) whenever I attempt to record a podcast or training video.

One more point on noise, especially for parents: If you've ever had younger kids in the house and had your own Parent Radar Spidey Senses go off at peak alert levels when they were suspiciously quiet, you might find that noise cancellation is *not* the answer. And while it's far from ideal, you might well have to blend parenting and working in ways nobody would choose from time to time, at the very least remaining alert to what other people are doing in the house while you are working, even if that work involves taking calls or listening to video/audio input. Furthermore, any of us may also need to listen for doorbells, oven timers, and other things which could have a legitimate call on our attention while working.

In that case, a different kind of headset might work for you: Bone conduction, behind the ear headphones, the ones cyclists use in traffic. These let you hear other sounds above whatever else is going on – at the same time not blocking out the warning signs of domestic disaster or those sudden, suspicious silences you really need to investigate.

If you need to hear an incoming call above the hubbub and make sure you don't miss critical communications, then adjusting your notifications could work, or something like a call alert light that grabs your attention and is physically clipped to the side of your monitor. When your soft phone app is buried behind seven other windows, all clamouring for your eyeballs, it might go unheard in a busy house. There are other ways to help the app to alert you, perhaps by vibrating your headset or something similar. Dig deep into its settings and see what you can find.

Sound quality and calls

While one positive legacy of the lockdown period is surely a far greater tolerance of domestic background noises and interruptions on calls, it's different with recorded sound, where a much higher standard is generally called for. I would really struggle to listen to a podcast or audiobook which had the same quality of sound as the average videoconference call, for example.

It's all a matter of expectation, and expectations change. Remember, for example, when mobile phones used very compressed bandwidth and signal, and you sounded like you were on a helicopter walkie talkie?

Younger readers won't know what I'm talking about, because nowadays you wouldn't put up with a mobile which sounded like that, or with having to regularly switch back to the landline when it all got too choppy. And I am sure that as working from home and conferencing online becomes more and more common, better quality audio will become the norm, and then the expectation. After all, it only takes one person with no headphones on a large group call, or someone with a background vacuum cleaner or horrible audible crackle, to seriously degrade the audio experience for the whole group.

If you are podcasting, delivering webinars, or just want to sound a heck of a lot better on calls, then invest in a decent standalone mic. My podcast engineer recommended a Blue Yeti to me, which some people hate. However, I find it's fine for my purposes. And if you and someone in the same room need to be in on the same call - I have found this more relevant for family stuff rather than work - you MUST use a headset. If you don't, your voice coming from their device is picked up by your mic again, and the echo, whine and general feedback unpleasantness builds up horrifically fast.

While it's worth spending more on good quality sound capture, i.e your microphone, the sound quality in your ears is less important. While you might choose headphones for various other qualities as discussed above, delivering high-end audio doesn't need to be a massive consideration, and the most expensive ranges tend to be optimised for listening to really well-mastered musical recordings. You simply won't notice enough of a difference, when you're listening to people talking, to justify a big price difference - at least in my opinion.

The other thing about anything pre-recorded is that this is the time to rigidly reinforce your audio boundaries at home. My house seems to be incredibly echo-filled and resonant - great for singing in the shower maybe, but not so much when someone closing a door a bit too firmly on another floor is picked up during a recording. So this is the one time when I am boringly strict and nagging about racket in the rest of the house. If I have to endure closed windows and no aircon, as well as physically blocking my lovely view from the (acoustically dreadful) glass terrace doors, then they can turn the TV down and not argue. They can definitely NOT interrupt me, unless the house is actually on fire. And even then, not till they've had a good shot at putting the fire out themselves first.

A friend with younger children than mine got her kids to design office door signage to help reinforce such boundaries. If the kids see the one with a volcano stuck on Mum's office door, they know they should really try not to bother her unless there's lava pouring on the floor, or a similarly urgent, life-threatening problem. (The monster picture means they can come in if they need to, but she is on an internal call or meeting with colleagues, so try not to interrupt. The only other time the door is closed, the smiley sun picture means Mum is concentrating and coding, and best interrupted only by someone bringing cake and tea… otherwise please tip-toe on past).

There are lots of creative ways to use sound to define and maintain your work from home boundaries, and we'll continue to discover more over time.

What you see is what you get

I mention above some of the most creative ways I have seen people carve out home offices in places which really didn't have obvious space for them. In many cases, this means one distinct area of compromise: your view. If you're working in the corner of a room, or under the stairs, you won't have a lot of visual inspiration.

That might be a good thing, in some ways. Having nothing to distract you from your work can create a hard visual boundary between you and the rest of the world that might otherwise tempt you to procrastinate, and when space is tight, it's unavoidable anyway. I used to have a home office that looked out into the garden, with the sea beyond it, which was lovely - but I am sure I spent a lot more time staring out of the window, out on the beach in my mind, than I should have during some work days or some work calls. And of course, wasted time in that way only kept me at my desk for longer in the end, leading inevitably to me spending less time out there where I really wanted to be.

When helping a client choose and design a space for working

from home, I will always recommend being close to a nice bright window if you can, because natural light is gentle on your eyes, and flattering to your appearance on a webcam too. However, being very close to the window might be simply too bright, and you could be better off seated to one side. All things being equal, even allowing for distraction, I will opt for a nice view if one is available - though it's a luxury that not every home can offer.

Another good choice for your line of sight are reminders of why you are working in the first place. Photos of your loved ones, or something your child drew or made for you, might help you grind on through a tough day. Or maybe you need a visual reminder of that beautiful holiday destination you're saving up for. You could create a full-blown vision board, to inspire your grafting towards longed-for goals. Maybe you'd feel self-conscious putting it on the wall in a shared office, but when you work from home you're the only one who will see it, and the only one who needs to see it.

Let there be light

I have seen people use combinations of natural and artificial light very creatively in home offices, and if you have a well-lit corner to work in, switching the light off before you log out for the day can help to cast it back into the shadows of your mind, where it belongs out of hours. I even heard from one woman who changes the light bulb in the corner of her living room to mark the end of the working day, and I think that is a really creative way to use a sensory condition to reinforce a task boundary.

As any interior designer can tell you, the way a room is illuminated makes a huge difference to its atmosphere, mood, and even what size and shape it appears to be. You can definitely use artificial lighting in a shared space to create a sense of work/not work zones, simply by hitting a switch. Bear in mind that the qualities of domestic lighting tend to be very different from office solutions, which are generally much more white and harsh than you would want at home. I am sure it's possible for your friendly neighbourhood electrician to rig up a clever switch to toggle between work and non-work illumination schemes that need not involve unscrewing bulbs twice a day.

You will also need to think about light in relation to webcam usage, if you have lots of meetings, or work with any kind of streaming or webcasting. Don't show up like some ghostly silhouette, especially if you want to feel like part of a team, rather than looking as if you're in witness protection. A good diffused light source shining on your face is a courtesy to your colleagues. Lots of YouTubers and similar folks use a ring light to create a soft focus on the face, but I can't get on with these due to permanent face-furniture: if you wear specs, any fixed light source facing you head-on will create distracting reflections on your lenses, and ring lights make you look like a robot from another galaxy.

For most business communications purposes, raising the ambient light in the room as a whole is the most flattering and effective solution. And investing in a half-decent external webcam, rather than relying on whatever microscopic device is bundled into the edge of your laptop, will make a big difference too.

Visible lines

Beyond light, visual boundaries can help to demarcate your 'work' space from 'home' when you don't have the luxury of a separate room. Floor coverings are one idea - maybe a rug can define your workspace, and when you step from it back into the main area of the room, you are no longer at work. And those horrible plastic mat things really do stop a wheely office chair from gouging grooves in your nice pile carpet.

In the vertical dimension, I have seen people manage a similar trick with curtains, including one cunning stairwell office which you would never know was there when it was hidden from view. When in use, the curtain slides right back on an extra-long rail, so it doesn't impinge on the workspace at all.

More flexibly, consider the use of room divider screens, as mentioned by a reader in the previous chapter. These can be inexpensive and lightweight, paper-covered and easy to store out of the way when not in use, but you can put them to work in all sorts of ways, including:

- Shielding a messy room behind you, with their plainness.

- Beyond that, obscuring the fact that you are working from home at all, or that you don't have a dedicated office and have had to set up shop in your bedroom temporarily.

- Separating the 'Office' from the 'Home-school' (though obviously, they are in no way sound proof…)

- Dividing a shared home office into two in a flexible way, for privacy and/or sanity.

- Diffusing a hard light source, as a translucent barrier.

- Creating a physical line that 'Shall not be crossed while Mummy is on a call.'

- Hiding your workspace from view when you're done for the day.

So, a simple bamboo and paper screen from IKEA or somewhere similar might be a good investment, even though you will have to store it when not actually in use. Remember, they can be bulkier than you'd imagine.

Touch, taste and smell

It might sound weird to some, but there are other ways you can bring sensory factors into your work-life boundaries in small but meaningful doses.

For example, coffee for me signals the start of the working day, and I know it is the aroma as much as the caffeine boost which comes to the aid of my productivity in that moment. There is a physical limit to how much of this wonderful stuff I can consume in one day for that reason, so I am quite ritualistic about, and try to use it to create a trigger for my most focused and creative work session. I have a friend who swears by an aromatherapy oil burner, and she uses specific blends to create a signal to her brain that it is now the working day. Something with geranium in it, I think, which correlates with concentration and focus for her.

I don't know about the scientific evidence supporting specific scents acting on your mind and body, but I do know there is a great deal of data supporting state-dependent memory and triggers, so it's well worth exploring if you have difficulty creating other sensory boundaries around your work space and activities. It's not about certain aromas doing things to your brain, it's about creating an association between creative and productive work, and a certain set of conditions. Think how powerfully connected with memory the sense of smell is, and this may resonate strongly for you.

It's well worth experimenting with all your senses, including touch - maybe avoiding that comfortable upholstery, while you're supposed to be in work mode, for example. And consider how you define the boundaries of your working day and location.

CHAPTER 4: TASK BOUNDARIES

Finding the edge between life and work

In the days before knowledge work was a thing, life was so much easier, at least in some ways.

When work consisted of showing up in a specific place for a given time period, and carrying on a particular quantifiable action, you knew exactly what to do - screw the widget into the hole, or put the topper on the cake, then move on and do the next one, until the bell rang for the end of your shift. Someone else designed the production line, and specified how you performed each action and in what order, and how that interrelated with what everyone else was doing. Your job was simply to, well, do your job, and you knew exactly what the outcome should look like, what was expected of you, and all the factors which could influence your work. Even if it was highly skilled and specialised in nature, your work had clearly defined edges, and everyone knew what it looked like when it was finished.

You didn't have to think about how you did it, or how you measured if it was done okay. You probably didn't stay late to finish screwing widgets into holes because you weren't sure if you'd done enough, and you probably didn't have nightmares and anxiety attacks about whether you were doing it right overall and progressing in your widget screwing career at the expected rate of change.

Knowledge work is totally different, and we need to strike a delicate and ongoing balance between planning, shaping and defining the work, and actually carrying it out. Even distinguishing between these two simple categories means using different parts of your mind, and that in itself is exhausting. We will take a deeper dive into this subject from the perspective of productivity in book 3.

It's particularly difficult when you work from home to recognise when you're 'done' - when your work is finished, for the day, for the month, or for the project. For this section, let's consider it from a boundaries point of view, in terms of establishing where the edge of your work is, and where the rest of your life begins.

Hard or soft edges?

If you were screwing widgets into holes, you knew exactly where work stopped. And even if your work was more complex than that, when you arrived at a particular building every day to do it, that in itself constituted an edge. Most people arrived around the same time and left the building around the same hour at the end of the working day.

Of course, you may have had targets and performance indicators to indicate how you were doing, and would have been subject to more formal appraisals and evaluations periodically, but you would probably have continued without more detailed feedback for long periods, while also realising you were putting in similar levels of effort, and generating similar levels of output, as your colleagues.

Once that was done, you could leave and not worry about

work till the following day. Your work was contained within a distinct space in your life, and the analogy of a fried egg can help illuminate this point. The yolk is essential -indeed integral to the meal - but it maintains a distinct boundary, while the rest of your life surrounds it, and can spread into the remaining available space in the pan.

As your career progressed and your responsibilities grew, it was natural for things to get a bit runnier and more blended, particularly with work bleeding into personal time and thoughts, if not the other way around. The yolk may have punctured and spread a bit, oozing into your discretionary time as notifications on your phone, or catch-up reading on the train home. It was a tendency you accepted as an inevitable part of the growing seniority of your career, with commensurate rewards, but it was still basically containable. Work happened at work, and life happened elsewhere.

For many people though, the removal of the travel and office boundaries by forced working from home has led to a full-on omelette situation, for which they found themselves totally unprepared. Does this sound familiar?

"How do I know if I have done enough today? What time did I start? What was I doing before and after I started work today, especially if it's all happening in the same place? If I have constant interruptions from my kids, I don't know where my work fits in with a shared progress target, I sense that maybe my manager thinks I am not coping or not being productive enough. And now I cannot find that edge any more.

At the very least, if we make an abrupt shift to working from home, life and work become lightly scrambled, perhaps for the first time in our working lives. And for many people, this can be inherently negative and damaging.

Integrators and Segmentors

Continuing with the egg analogy, we all take our eggs in different ways by preference, don't we?

Research by Nancy Rothbard published in Harvard Business Review in July 2020 framed the extremes of this spectrum of preference for work-life blend and distinction as **integrators vs segmentors**. It's a useful lens through which to explore the importance of this boundary, as well helping to understand why and how others you work with might see things totally differently, and cope in contrasting ways.

Basically, Integrators love to mix things together, scramble the egg into a million hues of yellow and orange, and find few distinctions between work time/space/activities and the personal side of things. Segmentors, on the other hand, prefer to keep things clearly in their own spaces and not mix things up at all.

Which are you? Do you feel more strongly drawn to one of these brief descriptions than the other?

I would locate myself quite strongly on the 'Integrator' side of the equation, and I am generally comfortable with blending life and work activities much of the time. Looking back to before I was self-employed, this makes sense for me as a long-term personality trait, as well as being somewhat inevitable in entrepreneurial life.

There are some personal times or situations where I construct clear boundaries and will not let work intrude, just as there are some work circumstances where I do my best to block out all interruptions from 'real life.' For the most part, though, I am fine with a high degree of overlap. If a personal call comes in during work time, that doesn't stress me out because I'll catch up later. Similarly, I don't mind checking work stuff during lulls in family or personal time, particularly if the ability to do so helps me enjoy more down time than a more rigidly structured life might afford. Lots of my personal reading informs my professional work, and I often make my family sit through geeky documentaries in which I have a work-related interest.

I have always enjoyed the chance to blend opportunities and seize serendipitous moments, which can only arise when you take this viewpoint, such as adding on a day or two of personal time to a business trip to a new location (incidentally, if we ever go back to business travel as a normal activity, can someone please come up with a better word than the unspeakable term 'Bleisure', for this practice?) Likewise, if a family trip took me near a client's location, I'd probably make time for a coffee to consolidate that relationship, if not a full-blown meeting.

Also, if I meet someone socially with whom I might have a professional interest in common, I'll probably be eager to discuss it, and if they are more of a Segmentor by nature, they might cut me off and suggest we fix up a call about this some other time: Picture the scene: "I mean really, you want to talk about APIs at Jo and Caroline's party...?" (Yes, I do!)

I usually work from my home office, but sometimes I will go to a coffee shop, or take a meeting in the garden, just to mix things up. Then I hear: "I love your Zoom background. Oh, it's one of those moving live ones, how cool!"

Back when I worked in someone else's office, I had pictures of my family on the wall, and work stuff lying around at home which I had taken back to read. As long as I was clear about my accountabilities and deliverables, I didn't really care when or where things got done. So perhaps a transition to (and high degree of fit with) home-based working was inevitable for me.

As it was, I probably talked much more about my life and family while at work than some of my colleagues did.

I have always had very clear boundaries about client and colleague relationships though, and the management of expectations there. I have more than once respectfully told a client *"No, I will not take a call at midnight to discuss your project"*, because even if they are half a world away, I consider 8 o'clock the cut-off point of reasonableness. They can even decide whether they are a morning or an evening person.

That said, I might still be thinking about their project late at night, and bookmarking something I will need to come back to later.

If you are reading this and thinking, 'Yes that's me!' we may well be fellow Integrators. However, if you're recoiling in horror at the sheer mixed up messiness of all this, then you may be way more Segmentorish than I am, though this is a spectrum rather than an either/or. However I do have some strict, though rarely articulated, rules about the kind of work I am happy to have bleed over into weekend catch ups or stolen moments during travel, compared with the type of activities I will only do while I know I am 'At Work'. So while I am highly integrated in many ways, I do have some segmentation and separation attributes, and we probably all do.

A Segmentor I once managed who also worked from home was completely different in her outlook and approach, and this model helps me to explain and assimilate some areas of difference and even misunderstanding which arose between the two of us over time.

I spoke to her once on a day she was having her home office desk replaced, and she sounded a little odd. "I'm sitting on the floor", she explained. Why on earth would she do that? I knew she had a comfortable home, with a selection of sofas and a kitchen table. She told me, "My old desk has been collected already, and the new one won't be delivered till later." She preferred to work sat on the floor with her phone and laptop arranged around her, rather than permit work to spread to anywhere else in her home.

She was also always absolutely on point about timing and attention to detail, 100% reliable and punctual - and not the sort of person I would ask to manage unpredictable client relationships or woolly, edgeless creative projects. She couldn't get started on projects if the clarity and boundaries she required weren't available on every aspect of the work from the outset. As her manager, I needed to be totally clear on the deliverables and expectations required, which I knew would be executed with unfailing accuracy.

While her workspace at home was very clearly defined, she hated video calls, and found them unnecessarily invasive. She was the only person I knew of on that team who regularly dressed smartly for work, because she found it helpful to have a different set of clothes and appearance for work vs. personal life.

Had she lived with my young family at the time, she might well have found their intrusions into the workspace and day unbearable, whereas I had to accept that blend from the outset and roll with it. One of the first bits of 'luxury' office equipment I insisted on 20 years ago -when this was high-tech and unusual - was a completely cordless phone for business calls. Those calls might have had to be taken from anywhere in the house, because in that house, a new-born also lived.

With this particular colleague, I had clear communication protocols established around emergency contacts. I had her personal mobile number safely noted too, in case I ever needed to reach her out of hours, because I knew with total certainty that she would be logged out of Slack and did not receive work related emails or any other kind of communication on her personal phone. But I would never have dreamed of using that number, outside of a genuine emergency.

She had long before chosen to work from home, and designed her life and space very contentedly around this choice. However, another Segmentor working from home reluctantly and/or in highly unsuitable circumstances is likely to be at risk of being very stressed and unhappy.

If you recognise yourself in this latter description, it could go some way towards explaining why you may find working from home more difficult than your partner, your housemates, or your colleagues who are doing similar work from their own homes. Even if you know they have no more space or time to work with than you, they may appear to have less stress and greater fluidity, just because of this difference in style.

And difference is all it is.

Being a Segmentor by nature is not a character flaw, and it can be a great asset - including, often, the ability to better switch off and disengage from difficulties at work, and in life generally. An Integrator is more likely to worry over a problem in moments when they cannot do anything whatsoever about it, whereas a Segmentor can better detach, and maintain focus around what they are currently occupied with. Segmentors can be tremendously productive, and if they prefer to bafflingly operate two different calendars or phones for life and work, then they are still less likely to muddle them up or leave them somewhere, than I am with just one.

Integrators who have high professional expectations of themselves, or have them imposed from elsewhere, might find it hard to log off and quit for the night. To impose a boundary of 'Done For Now' if their work Slack is binging away, or emails are popping up on their phone during dinner can be particularly problematic.

A little self-knowledge can help you to analyse potential points of tension and consider tactics for reducing pain and stress by taking your known propensity into account. Wherever you find yourself on this spectrum, you will be happiest if you can bring your working style and habits into alignment with your needs.

Boundary maintenance tips for Segmentors

- If you feel better dressing for work, go for it! So long as you're not uncomfortable, anything goes when working at home, and you should follow your own inclinations.

- If you feel awkward about over-sharing on video calls, think about rearranging and depersonalising your space. While many people love the windows into the lives of others that a view of a book case or artwork choice signifies, you have total control about what is within shot, because it's your home. For a quick neutral option, grab a cheap folding room divider screen to literally segment off your space, as discussed above.

- Work in the same place at home, at the same time, using the same tools if you can, just to keep your boundaries clear.

- Make sure you are completely clear about the accountabilities and deliverables which define your daily work. Do whatever you can to reduce any ambiguities that might create uncertainty.

- Pre-empt interruptions during work time, negotiating with those with who you share a home in advance if necessary.

- Even if your work is totally flexible, you might find it useful to block your schedule clearly in advance, constraining the times other people can book you for meetings, for example, and making certain everyone knows you finish and log off early on Thursday to take your kid to basketball.

- Ask your employer, or structure your self-employment, to keep your apps and tools distinct. Even if your employer operates a 'bring your own device' policy, it's not unreasonable for them to provide something like a separate laptop for you to do your work on, for example. It's a great deal easier for the IT department to control and secure it too. Or set up a separate virtual desktop, if you need to use the same machine for different purposes.

- Choose the level of deliberate sharing and disclosure that YOU feel comfortable with at work, and don't let anyone pressure you into feeling you have to bring personal stuff into the workplace, if that isn't within your comfort zone. Working remotely gives you total control over this aspect of your life.

Boundary maintenance tips for Integrators

- Get clear in your mind, and/or with your manager, what 'Done' looks like, on any given project or area of work.

- Ritualise your start and end to the day, to give it some edges (see below). The ending is particularly important, because that is when the bulk of your personal time is likely to be enjoyed.

- Figure out some dealbreakers and state them, clearly and politely. I insist on scheduling calls with my West coast clients during their morning only, not at their convenience through the day, which could wind up in the middle of the night here in Europe.

- Log out of, or manage alerts on, work related apps and tools, especially if you know you will not be able to resist looking at them out of hours if they're there to tempt you with those little red dots.

- Talk about communication plans and strategies with your colleagues, and even your family/housemates. What is urgent, what is important, what kind of communication is appropriate under what circumstances? We'll go into this in more detail in a later book, but for now, think about: kids, don't interrupt me in the office if you can hear I am on a Zoom, unless it's really urgent. Don't do an @team Slack message out of hours, unless the server is down or there's a big data breach... Etc.

The edges of the day

It's worth remembering that even in the typical shared office, the working day edges have been steadily eroding for some time now.

Back in the distant 20th century past, when I commuted to central London, the one thing I looked forward to was reading on the train. Escapist fiction as a rule, an expensive habit given my long journey, and doubtless responsible for the honourable demise of many a tree. We didn't have eBooks or games on our phones back then. But even if I couldn't get a seat and had to read crammed up into someone's armpit, it was still my time, to escape by any means.

That's not so much the case nowadays.

My last few visits to London have demonstrated a transition from mobile device peering to a proliferation of full-sized laptops wedged uncomfortably on to tray tables on commuter trains, with the rail service thoughtfully providing both WiFi and even power sources to support this. A lack of regard for even basic privacy and security awareness makes it abundantly clear that the majority of my fellow travellers are typically reading and replying to emails, or working on reports and spreadsheets, as they are whisked into their city offices for the day.

Once there, they are in danger of contracting the nasty workspace ailment of presenteeism - something which homeworkers are NOT immune to I hasten to add, and end up making sure they're not the last to leave, while heading back with a pile of reading and late messages to get through on their journey home.

Even a few years ago, when people were usually on their

phones instead of clutching newspapers and novels, there was at least a chance they were doing their own thing and choosing where to focus their attention. This laptop thing is clearly work, work, work, though, with no let up, and it's a shame.

I have no suggested cure for this state of affairs beyond the obvious, but I mention it as a point to consider, if you are struggling to find a clear start and end to the homeworking day. Even if people in offices are typically spending two or three hours more working than you are, at least they're more likely to close the laptop when they get off the train and not open it again until the following morning. The act of going to a designated room in a work building does impose a boundary of some sort, that is frequently lost when working from home.

After all, while most contracts of employment -when did you last read yours, if you have one? - specify a certain number of working hours per week, in most executive roles this is superseded by a shared understanding of full-time commitment, whatever form that may take. In practice, this means something loosely modelled on the 9-5 working day, which worked so well when we all stood at the production line cranking widgets, and it also means not doing other kinds of work - including personal stuff - at the same time.

For the cheerfully integrated homeworker though, the day might start with a blend of personal and professional activities; listening to the financial news while going for a jog, or checking emails as you feed kids and put the laundry on. There could be tasks specifically around transforming space from 'Home' into 'Office' mode, such as clearing down tables or putting the day's coffee to brew.

And at the end of the day, whenever that is, you might have to do the reverse and restore shared areas, as well as starting to let more of the domestic stuff in. That's if it hasn't been blending its way through your work all day, with a mixture of home-schooling, signing for deliveries and getting distracted by domestic tasks.

What does work expect?

If you're employed and/or working as part of a team, there will be other people's work patterns and expectations to consider too. This is further complicated by the 2020 transition to remote work, that often came about in a chaotic and non-strategic way.

When you all sat in the office together, you may never have had a conversation about normal and expected start and end times, because looking around you provided all the information you needed about what was normal in your workplace. If someone wasn't at their desk during the middle of the day, the assumption would be that they were gainfully engaged on work-related business elsewhere, such as being in a meeting -you remember, '*going to meetings*'. If you sent an email, or even if you used a team-wide messaging service like Slack, no one worried if someone didn't reply immediately, because you could look up and see they were stuck on a long phone call, or head down in a complex spreadsheet.

Maybe some people played games - a jacket on the back of a chair, never leaving until at least one minute after the manager. There were all sorts of ways to signal your diligence and engage in presenteeism. Some people will translate those games to the remote workspace by checking out documents really late in the day, replying to emails at strange hours of the day and night, or feeling obliged to frequently mention the long hours they've been putting in or lengths they have gone to.

If you're the team leader/manager you need to consider

whether this is the kind of behaviour you want to acknowledge and reward, because it's rarely healthy. It could signal a personal time management problem you'll want to address via individual feedback and review, and it could also point to a broader sense of lack of acknowledgement and visibility within the team, which also needs fixing. While it's outside the scope of this book, you might find *Thinking Remote: Inspiration for Leaders of Distributed Teams* helpful on this front.

Whether or not you are in a formal leadership role, I encourage you to explore ways to make your accomplishments and your boundaries visible to your colleagues, both peers and managers, because it will help you find YOUR edge. If no one is doing this for you, take the initiative - *that's project X task B sorted, so I am logging off now, night night all!*

Communication clarity

In more typical times, were a team to transition to home-based or otherwise office-optional working, there would ideally be some norms agreed and defined about how we 'Come to work' - for example, do we shout up in a Slack channel to say we're here and now working for the day, or do we assume that people will be around from X to Y o'clock unless clearly specified in advance?

What if we're going to be unavailable to others for a while? We also need to know what both the official policy *and* - if it varies - any unspoken norms around this are.

It might help to imagine yourself explaining this to someone new joining the team, because at some point you will likely need to do just that. Write it all down as a starting point for codifying into some kind of team agreement or protocol, and you might even discover that different team members are starting from radically different assumptions about all this stuff and are working to maintain different kinds of boundaries around your team connections and communications. For example:

- When sending a message to the main team Slack channel, how soon do we expect people to respond?

- Is that expectation different, depending on who sends it?

- What about if it's an email instead?

- If I am going to be in a meeting for an hour, should I mention it to my colleagues? Is putting it in a shared diary/calendar app sufficient, so they can see for themselves where I am? Or is it none of their business, and I'll simply get back to them on my return/when it's convenient?
- Do I still do this if I am just going to be muting messages for a while to get on with a deeply focused bit of work?

- What about if I am going to a personal appointment instead?

- Am I asking people, including my manager, or telling them?

- What length of absence or reply is going to trigger them to think, 'Hmm I wonder where on earth he is?' - and are we expected to raise our hand and excuse ourselves from the flow of conversation if we need to go to the bathroom?

- Do we have ways to signal our engagement with something really quickly and frictionlessly? Like responding to a Slack message or even an email with an emoji you mutually agree means 'Yep I have read this, broadly agree, and suggest no further action'?

- How do we say 'I just arrived at work, hello everyone!' - Do we need to say that? Is one person doing this to check in and connect personally with colleagues on an emotional level, while someone else is 'taking a class register' and noticing who is 5 minutes later than everyone else?

None of these questions have one-size-fits-all-teams answers, and cultural norms will evolve in remote teams just as they do in face-to-face groups. However, it's easy for inexperienced managers who have had no training in how to manage people remotely to come to be overly dependent on 'Messaging Presenteeism.'

They may develop powerless paranoia around the idea of time theft, and worrying about what people are doing when they cannot see them, while frequently failing to appreciate that if someone is sat in meetings and messaging them back all day, they're probably getting very little else done as a consequence.

In order to develop a shared understanding around this, it's really valuable to have a conversation, and create some kind of agreement around how to use each communication channel appropriately, depending on its context and urgency, and who it's relevant for.

Yes, a lot of this is common sense. You won't WhatsApp the CEO to explain you're popping out to the supermarket, negotiate your salary on a public message thread, or email the fire brigade when your house is burning down. Other things might be less obvious though, or present differently to different people, and knowing exactly how to communicate a specific fact - what medium to use, to whom, any particular escalations or conditions - can create a lot of reassurance in any work environment.

CHAPTER 5: RITUALS AND ROUTINES

One person I recently spoke to, who has adjusted well to working from home, was nonetheless wistful about something which sounded on the face of it surprising. He missed his commute to work.

Angelo is a senior administrator in education policy living in Sussex, near London. His role involves demanding responsibilities but rarely bleeds into out-of-hours time. Mornings were always about a brisk cycle to the station, followed by a relaxing hour on a not terribly overcrowded train. Living so far from the city meant a long journey, but a guaranteed seat with a table, where he enjoyed checking messages, but also catching up on the daily news and social media, over a cup of good coffee from the carpark cafe. After disembarking from the train in a very different place physically and emotionally from where he started, a five minute stroll along the South Bank completed the transition into his working day. He was now embedded in that unique London culture he first enjoyed as a student decades before, which had always inspired and energised him.

Since working from home, he had regained literally hours for himself every week, not to mention saving money on the season ticket, the coffee shop, and all those second-hand book stalls on the South Bank. Yet he felt like he had lost something, an important part of the ritual which created the edge of his working day and mindset. Despite the time he'd reclaimed to enjoy in his beautiful semi-rural home and community, he found himself procrastinating, and frequently starting work *later* than when he used to take that early train.

Part of the problem arose from the impact on mood and wellbeing of missing that cycle ride, which was an important part of his exercise regime in most weather conditions, so replacing that was essential. But it was bigger than that, and it took us a little while to come up with the right solution for him to try out: the "Virtual Commute".

Angelo now starts each day with a brisk walk into the village, where he visits a different coffee shop and buys the paper, sitting outside to read it when weather permits, or bringing it home to enjoy in the living room of his comfortable cottage. His walk takes him in the opposite direction to the station but still gives him some exercise to start the day, which is usually supplemented by a bike ride in the early afternoon, which seems to be a time of energy slump and reduced concentration at his desk anyway.

Ritualising the movement, the media engagement, and the caffeine intake, and replacing these in a new context, has created a specific boundary to the working day. Just like on the train, he makes a point of not checking emails on his phone while he reads the paper, because he's always had a healthy sense of that kind of boundary between work and life.

What he was lacking in the early days of working from home was a way of delineating time at work from time to himself, especially first thing in the morning, and he needed to find a way to ease between the two states of mind. Sure, he could have read the news electronically, or bought a fancy home espresso machine with a fraction of his savings on that season ticket. However, they represented more than the sum of their parts, and identifying this meant a significant uplift in his peace of mind, and his ability to rock on without procrastination.

Miraculous mornings (and evenings)

Of course, having a morning routine is far from an original idea.

In his bestseller, The Miracle Morning, Hal Elrod talks about an optimised morning routine which he has researched and tested to combine the most effective way to prime your mind and body. He proposes a seven-step system, complete with the handy acronym SAVERS, consisting of Silence (meditation or prayer), Affirmations (positive self-talk), Visualisations (seeing things as you want them to be and being very clear about the future you want to create), Exercise (of any kind), Reading (learning something), and Scribing (by which he means journalling or daily pages).

This is a powerful framework which many people have found success with, and it's well worth experimenting with, to see if you can adapt it to fit your lifestyle. Elrod is a highly successful ultra-marathoner, salesman, and speaker, who has overcome astonishing life challenges and conducted extensive research into the morning routines of some of the world's most productive and effective people to create this model. It's spawned a vast online following, as well as multiple spin-off titles, and a feature length documentary.

Some have criticised this approach, pointing out they simply don't have time to do all seven things in the morning, and while the author suggests that even a minute of each is worthwhile, this critique has some validity for me in terms of realistic expectations.

Every item on the list will bring you benefits, but if you find you prefer to journal and reflect at the end of the day, or go for a swim at lunchtime when the gym membership is cheaper off peak or whatever, then you don't need to tick all seven boxes before you start work, in my opinion, to benefit. While the book includes some useful affirmations and self-talk to encourage earlier rising and ways to view yourself as a morning person which can be very powerful, the reality in my experience is that not everyone can reprogram their circadian rhythms in this way. As such, you might end up trying to do all this while not at your mental peak, or when they are competing for your peak with other essential high-powered tasks. And many people, even those who work from home, frequently have other constraints to manage, like kids to get to school.

It's well worth taking a look at though because some of the SAVERS can be done briefly or even overlapping one another, like reading through a list of affirmations, or reviewing a visualisation. You could make a slideshow on your phone for example, using positive words and images of your dreams combined, to condense the two, or listen to audiobooks while you go for a walk. And if you gain even a small uptick in your productivity and creativity, you might eventually find you need fewer hours at your desk to achieve the same work output - which is a win-win situation.

The science of habit

Certainly, Elrod is not alone in identifying the evidence for starting the day with a routine, and enjoying the physiological and psychological benefits it can bring. Tim Ferriss's Tribe of Mentors book and his podcast interviews frequently discuss the way very high achievers in a diverse range of fields start their day, and routine seems to be a common trait in those who have achieved big things in their lives, both personally and professionally.

Investor and author James Altucher has written extensively about his morning practice, which he credits with literally saving his life on more than one occasion. This includes daily exercise, i.e. moving enough to break a sweat for at least 10 minutes, connecting emotionally by helping people who uplift you and avoiding those who don't, some form of prayer or spiritual practice, and mental stimulation. This can take the form of listing ideas, something I have often incorporated into my own daily routine. The brain might not be a muscle physiologically, but it behaves in similar ways, and warming it up and the idea of 'use it or lose it' certainly applies.

You can see common themes in all of these routines, especially around physical exercise, emotional tuning to set yourself up positively for the day, and a reflective component in which you get in touch with your innermost self or a higher power of choice. None were designed specifically for working from home, but lots of successful people are using routines like this to get themselves into the right frame of mind to be happy, productive, and creative – so you can too.

Establishing habits isn't easy though, and there is contradictory evidence around how many times you need to repeat things before they become ingrained, and the power of different tricks you can play on yourself to make something 'stick'. From my own experience and all I have learned from comparing different approaches, a few things are clear.

Making shifts in our behaviour is difficult – so:

Take small steps

If adopting an hour-long, multi-stage morning routine is overwhelming, try adding one thing. Even if you stick a post-it note on your bathroom mirror with 3 positive affirmations written down to look at while you brush your teeth, it's a start. Just like when you decide you want to lose weight or train for a marathon, you can't change everything at once, so you need to take one step at a time.

Nevertheless, even while your changes in behaviour are small, it's important to be completely clear about your reasons for making them. It's easier to make an excuse for not doing your morning journalling if you don't understand or embrace that it matters because it helps to stimulate and unleash your creativity. Remember, if you have shifted from commuting to working from home, you HAVE regained time - so why not put it to positive personal use?

Stack the successes

If you want something to become part of your 'normal', then set yourself up to keep track of it. What gets measured gets managed remains true, even if this wasn't the original context of the saying. Put a tick in your diary each time you do your morning meditation or run. How long can you make the chain? Jerry Seinfeld made a commitment early in his career to write one joke every day, and each time he did so he put a cross on his calendar, as a visual reminder of the hours he was putting in and the consistency he was achieving.

The effect can be really powerful, and personal, because it means something to you even if to nobody else. I remember my husband thought I was joking when I WhatsApped him from an overseas conference, demanding not only that he ticked off my achievement of my daily step count on a chart on the wall in my office at home, but also send me a photo of the tick in its place in line. It meant a something to me, in a way that ticking them all off together when I got home would not have had the same impact.

Of course, there is a danger here that the one day the wheels come off and you don't do the thing, you feel like everything's collapsed and gone to hell, so and you might as well quit and give it up. Think ahead to what will happen when you do miss your target, and be ready to get right back on the horse.

Promise yourself that you'll never permit more than one day's break in the chain, then any time you miss your mark will result in increased motivation rather than despondency.

Stack the habits

Doing the affirmations in your head in the bathroom? Great. Now decide to add a 5 minute meditation in afterwards. Look for a beginner app you like the feel of, such as Headspace, Calm, Balance or FitMind, and take out a trial subscription, or just set a timer on your phone and breathe mindfully for a short time. Pair it with something you always do anyway, like sitting down with your coffee - could you focus on your breath instead of your phone for that first five minutes?

Could you listen to an educational podcast or audiobook during that 20 minute walk? Maybe you can start by adding the walk, while the coffee machine heats up for the day.

Anchoring a new habit to an existing one is compelling and effective, because the one that's already in place becomes the trigger to remind you about the new habit.

Experiment and test

Not ready to commit to the year-long ultramarathon yet? Me neither, so any new exercise routine must not only start from where we find ourselves right now, the finish line has to be realistic too. Picking the right level of challenge is important:

too easy and you won't bother, but an end in sight really helps.

Right now, I am doing a 30-day Spanish language challenge, and I am almost halfway through. It's about irregular verbs, and it's horrible - because my Spanish grammar is terrible. I really need to learn it, but I hate it, only slightly less than I hate my terrible incompetence in my ability to communicate in the country I have chosen to live in, so I am determined to chip away at it. That's why I was so glad to come across this 30-day course, which releases a few minutes of new material each day, and is only supposed to take 15 minutes to complete.

1% of my day, to improve my Spanish? (Alright, 1.04% for the pedants, but this is Spanish not maths!) OK I can commit to that, but only because it's just a month long. And even if I feel like all these conjugations are going in one ear and out the other at least I am being exposed to them daily, in a way that as a home-based writer (in English) simply doesn't happen, unless I make it so.

If I'd signed up for an hour a week for a year, I'd probably have quit the first time I had a difficult deadline, and yes, I speak from a position of repeated experience on this. But one month? I can do that! So can you. It's not changing your life, it's just running a little test. A sprint, rather than a marathon.

Incidentally, at the time of writing, I am failing somewhat on the habit stacking front with this course, because I am not being consistent about when I do it. After writing this chapter and reflecting on why it's proving a struggle to get done - and ticked off on my planner, of course- I see the problem. It's going to work a lot better if I can get clear with myself that I must do this BEFORE I open my inbox, or AFTER I do my meditation, or something specific to embed it in my routine, or letting it bleed into work time. You can ask me in the Healthy Happy Homeworking Facebook group if I managed to sort that out and get to the end of the month!

I am deliberately leveraging the power and momentum of the sprint to get through all these horrible verbs, while being very aware that this can be an expensive way to buy self-study material. Because the only training course that matters is the one you actually complete.

You will find lots of '30-day challenges' online, particularly in the exercise category, so you can try this for yourself. Sometimes trainers release them as loss-leading introductions to their longer programmes, so it's a great way to get a feel for their style, while you achieve rock steady abs or perfect your subjunctives, as the mood takes you. And you can always buddy up with someone for accountability - come and find a partner in the Healthy Happy Homeworking group if you need that extra bit of motivation.

Evening rituals and routines

It isn't just the mornings that matter, and you can use the power of habit to help you switch *out* of work mode and back into YOU mode when you're done for the day. If you have a habit of taking your work home with you when you work from home, even in your head, how you end the day could be one of your most important boundaries to establish and maintain.

Productivity writer and guru Cal Newport, author of the highly recommended Deep Work and many other titles, has a specific practice for the end of his working day. After going through a series of steps to capture any outstanding loops and unfinished business, things he needs to pin down before the following day or get onto a list or calendar - we'll come back to all these tools and tactics in book 3 - he speaks aloud the phrase

'Shutdown Complete'.

No one else can hear him, but he hears himself, consciously and sub-consciously - and he knows what it means. He won't utter the phrase until work is done for the day with nothing further to worry about, nothing to take away from his desk to nag away in the back of his mind. It's all there, waiting for the morning, and it can be dealt with then, creating a deliberate, defined edge between the end of the work day and the beginning of the non-work evening. He knows, deep down where it counts, that he won't say the words out loud until they're factually true, so when he hears himself say them, they work for him.

Then he can relax, so the following day, he can work better:

"If you keep interrupting your evening to check and respond to e-mails, or put aside a few hours after dinner to catch up on an approaching deadline, you're robbing your directed attention centers of the uninterrupted rest they need for restoration. Even if these work dashes consume only a small amount of time, they prevent you from reaching the levels of deeper relaxation in which attention restoration can occur. Only the confidence that you're done with work until the next day can convince your brain to downshift to the level where it can begin to recharge for the next day to follow. Put another way, trying to squeeze a little more work out of your evenings might reduce your effectiveness the next day enough that you end up getting less done than if you had instead respected a shutdown."

— Cal Newport, Deep Work: Rules for Focused Success in a Distracted World

I do something similar but less ritualised at the end of the day, making sure my inbox is dealt with, and my known priority tasks and fixed appointments for the morning are clearly noted on my schedule. Both on paper and in my task manager of choice, I make sure that everything that was on my list for the day is either rescheduled/deferred to another date, or ticked off firmly as *done* - then I close the lid of my laptop (which I will do anything to avoid using for personal matters out of work time, to the point of tapping out long messages on my iPad by preference).

I don't say anything out loud, but I know this ritual means work is completed, and my mind is free to log itself off for the evening. Depending on the season/weather, this is generally followed by a walk or a swim, though it can be straight to the couch in the dark dead of winter, but only for reading, conversation, TV, and downtime though. Work is finished.

You can co-opt others to support your rituals, like letting your kids know you're done and ready to play at last, or let them stream freely on your overstretched internet connection.

Nadine from the Healthy Happy Homeworking Facebook group ends her day by taking her dogs for a walk - and they are very good at reminding her it's time to stop and walk away from her desk, when the moment comes. It's really important to fit exercise into your work-from-home day somehow or other, and it might work better for you at the end of the day instead, whether you want to boost your energy to enjoy the evening, blow away a day's cobwebs, or burn off stress with a high energy cardio session.

Naturally it's very tempting to mark the boundary of professional vs personal time with a glass of something incompatible with work, and for many people this ritualistic Rioja or whatever will be a very healthy and consistent way of ending the day. For others though, it could signal a relationship with alcohol which is easily becoming dependent and toxic, if you end up in a place where you *need* that drink in order to switch off from work.

While I almost never drink alcohol myself now, I did for many years and you'll get no judgement from me. My morning coffee ritual could be considered just as much chemical dependency, and you're an adult making your choices. Just keep an eye on things, and test/challenge your routine from time to time to see how much you are in control of it, as opposed to the other way around.

Whatever you decide on for your evening ritual, I recommend finding some kind of closure or ending point on the work front which means you park things in a way you can easily reconnect with them the following morning. This is because of the *Zeigarnik effect*, in which it is demonstrated that tasks which are unfinished or interrupted may be more easily recalled (whether or not you want them to be).

Russian psychologist Bluma Zeignarnik studied restaurant waiters, who maintained incredible recall of customer orders on outstanding bills - but struggled to remember even what the customer had eaten as soon as the bill was paid. Their subconscious held tight to the unfinished business, then promptly let it go the moment it was no longer relevant. So when you have something you meant to finish but didn't, or something which came up but you didn't capture somewhere you'll see it again, it creates a specific cognitive tension which makes it more accessible to you in future - whether you want it to be or not. You know the feeling, when you know you need to remember something or do something important, but you can't get to it right now, so it churns away at the edge of your mind taking up far more space than it deserves.

This is why, if I have something in my daily list that I don't get done, I deliberately re-date it. I am going to do it tomorrow now, so I can let go of it tonight. I live and die by my lists so if something is there for the morning, I know I will be reliably reminded of it then, and my subconscious knows I don't need to keep worrying at it all night. Of course you can't necessarily switch your brain off completely if you're still not sure what you, are going to do with the task when morning comes, but at least you're not also trying to remember it exists. This really does work - if you try nothing else, try this one idea.

Routines in reality

In the morning, I have a flexible start up ritual comprising a range of activities from meditation to exercise. The exact nature of this is dependent on my schedule, my mood, my priorities and my state of mind, but I always do *something* between getting dressed and sitting at my desk Something that's not housework or domestic stuff, but I take a few moments at least to focus on myself and my own needs, and put in some kind of edge. In the past, I used to deal with email and social media on my phone in bed, but ditching this has improved my life in immeasurable ways, and I urge you to consider trying it for yourself.

Obviously, my mornings and evenings - just like yours - involve non-fun domesticity as well, and for many people the 'second shift' of parenting, caring, cooking, and cleaning is every bit as demanding as the working day just ended. Creating a buffer of some kind between the two can help however, if only to shift gears from one headspace into the other, and ensure that as much as possible, concern about the other role doesn't continue to preoccupy and dominate.

In knowledge work in particular, we are frequently dealing with wave after wave of new information and learning, and taking a little bit of time to reflect on learning helps to embed and consolidate it. Research bears this out, indicating that when learning a new role in particular, spending 15 minutes of reflection at the end of each day leads to 20% better performance than for those who instead spent the time on active practice.

Work also creates stress, which builds up in the body physically and adrenally, so taking time to reflect on what you have accomplished, and noting down what you've learned, earned, or done - you know what matters to you most - might help bring a sense of having won the day and succeeded. An evening ritual of mindful breathing, scanning the body for areas of tension, or a few simple yoga stretches, can get the kinks out of body and soul.

It's not just for you either - the people you share your life and home with may appreciate the company of a less stressed-out you. A you who has learned ways to leave some of the tension hormones at the desk, and reconnect with empathy and relaxation mindsets in which you can all enjoy each other's company more.

The importance of a virtual commute has been recognised by Microsoft Teams, who are planning to incorporate the concept into their toolset in a future update - it isn't quite certain what this will look like, but I'll be sure to let you know at http://healthyhappyhomeworking.com/admin/tech-updates/ once we know more.

In the meantime, here are a selection of ideas from which to build your own morning and evening rituals:

Morning ritual elements:

- Stretching and moving, yoga or pilates

- Downing a big glass of water (Okay, I prefer mine blasted at high temperature through ground coffee beans, but hydration matters as well)

- Meditation

- Affirmations

- Visualisation (over any timeframe, from nailing this day or a tricky upcoming event, to future dreams)

- Reviewing your life goals in your planner or notebook, reconnecting with your WHY in whatever form you have recorded it

- Connecting with your god or higher power of choice

- Exercise to raise the heart rate

- Planning the day (or longer), in an app or on paper

- Dressing in a particular way if it helps

- Cold water (either a blast in the shower Wim Hof style, or the achingly trendy wild swimming)

- Listening to uplifting music

- Writing a list of 10 ideas on a theme

- Journalling / freewriting

- A non-work-related learning activity

- Reviewing work commitments and defining your most important task to get done first, and/or your big three goals for the day.

Evening ritual elements:

- Collecting and listing unfinished tasks and commitments, putting them into a trusted system for recall at the time and place you intend to deal with them. (From an app-based task management list to a post-it note on your desk for morning)

- Checking in and reporting progress/accomplishments to your manager or team

- Tidying up your workspace (physically and virtually)

- Stretching and bending, postures to counterbalance the desk-bound hunched shoulders

- Gratitude journaling

- Going for a walk

- Reflection on learning

- Closing your laptop

- Talking to someone not about or related to your work

- Changing out of 'work' clothes

- Getting into a new physical environment (e.g. out of doors, or just a different room)

- A reward food/beverage (while being mindful of the possible dependency risks here)

Try taking two or three from each list, and mixing and matching with your own ideas, to create your own start-up and shut-down rituals for the work-from-home day. Then maybe add journalling, to reflect on how well this is working for you, and tweak and adjust things as you go along. Remember, this is for your own benefit, unless you are required to log completed tasks to satisfy someone else, so make sure you do things mindfully and meaningfully.

CHAPTER 6: TECHNOLOGY AND OUR BOUNDARIES

Enslaved to the red dot

If working from home has freed you from the tyranny of the morning commute, you may get to start the day in a more leisurely way than before, lingering in bed with the first tea or coffee of the day, and fondly reflecting on dashing to the bus stop in days of yore.

However, the chances are nowadays that cosy moment will be accompanied by a pocket-sized device that you reach for even before the coffee cup. After all, it's in your hand from the moment you silence the alarm clock, which is one of its featured apps.

Which of the little red notification alerts on your homepage will grab your attention first? Has someone tagged you, liked a post, sent you a direct message? How about an email? If you have a widget on your home-screen that tells tales on you, which app does it suggest is 'commonly used on first pickup?' Maybe you're driven by on-screen notifications, or perhaps you prefer to look directly at the pages of apps themselves.

Each little interaction, each little like, will feed you a tiny stab of dopamine, which provides a different kind of stimulation to the caffeine and tannins in your mug. It's compelling and addictive, and just like that morning jolt of coffee, it creates its own escalating feedback loop, requiring ever higher numbers of

RTs or DMs to trigger the same effect as time goes by. It lands squarely in your brain's reward centre – which incidentally is the same place as chocolate and sex.

However, the inventor of Facebook's Like button, Justin Rosenstein, publicly deleted the app (and others similar) from his phone, due to the psychological affects he was all too well aware of. The unintended consequences of 'doom-scrolling,' and the connection between mental health and overuse of social media apps is a matter of public record. Attention is the only non-scalable asset in the new economy, and the innovators in Silicon Valley will stop at nothing to keep you coming back more often, and spending more and more time looking at that screen.

This is bad enough for your friend stories and cat videos, but the trouble is, when it comes to the apps we use for work collaboration, the big trend is to make them more and more like our familiar social tools.

This is great from a usability perspective, as it minimises the learning curve and makes it easy to onboard new people. If you join a new team or organisation, there is a vast range of tools and interfaces they may be using - but it's pretty strong odds you'll immediately recognise certain features like emoji reactions, threaded conversations, usernames, @-tagging of specific individuals or themes, and so on. The app might have a different icon - which for some reason will probably be blue and white - but the way it points your attention to different content and lets you slip comfortably right into the conversation will feel natural and familiar.

Your team might use even Facebook Workplace, perhaps the ultimate in this social-workspace mash-up, or somebody may have hit on the terrible option of using consumer-based social apps for remote collaboration anyway, "Because everybody's already got WhatsApp, right?" As a freelancer, obviously it's my job to fit in with whatever the client already does, assuming they've hired me to write rather than to consult on their ecosystem. I have seen it all, including a cross-continental fintech start-up wholly reliant for team conversation on a single WhatsApp chat, largely filled with different styles of cat emojis. It's just wrong, on so many levels.

This familiarity with apps helps you engage with new tools quickly, but it also helps you immediately import your personal default settings and expectations on an emotional level, with all the baggage this evokes.

Because of this convergence of appearance, functionality, and how we respond with our feelings, when we pick up our phones in the morning, our work instant messaging app can have just as strong a pull on our attention as our social media feeds. Look at all those red dots... how can you possibly resist a quick tap, even though your manager isn't out of her pyjamas yet, and no one's paying you for your time right now?

This combination of the psychological tricks of the attention economy and the convergence of business and social apps we use means there's every danger of seriously eroding our boundaries, especially when it comes to tech and communications apps. Your personal placement on the integrator-separator spectrum discussed above will play a big part in your degree of comfort with this. That said, it's vital to be aware of it and in control, rather than letting other people's expectations or an installer's default settings rule your life - and your phone - in this way.

Just as we talked about how you can stack habits together to add behaviours you want to cultivate to those you already do without thinking in the previous chapter, the app providers want to do this for you by hooking your actions to your everyday tools and behaviours. To deny them this victory, you need to act directly and specifically in the opposite direction.

Here are some things to experiment with:

Master your notifications

This isn't just about the work tech, incidentally. I hate to make ageist generalisations, so I won't mention what it's like hanging out with certain more mature friends and relatives, who have expensive high-end phones, that are quite literally all singing-all-dancing. Lighting up like a Christmas tree and binging and buzzing every few minutes, there are serious personal etiquette issues for a start, but these can all be resolved by spending a few moments digging into the notification settings, on an app-by-app basis. *Just give me two minutes with your damn phone...*

I was with someone the other day whose wrist suddenly flashed a Slack icon while he was having dinner. He didn't react, so I pointed it out, assuming that any channel or combination of tags that actually pushed to his Apple Watch after 8pm would be the equivalent of the building being on fire, but he said no, he received all his Slack messages on his watch, and hadn't yet figured out how to turn them off. Arghh! Naturally, his phone was covered in enticing red, numbered blobs in the corner of every other app - so how could he possibly relax out of work time - and also, how could anyone be confident of getting his attention if there actually *were* a fire?

Any app, certainly if it's built for business use, has highly granular and user-configurable alerts and notifications. Have a good dig through yours and decide what you actually want to get in your face (or the faces of your dining companions), and when and how you want it to happen. You can decide, at the levels of channels, tags/being called out by name, by the status you set, and by what your normal office hours are.

They're your tech toys, they probably weren't cheap, and they're supposed to make your life better. Do spend some time setting them up how you want, and keep this under review, especially as new software updates can override your carefully-configured protocols. If you enjoy this newfound peace, you can do the same with your Facebook and WhatsApp, incidentally.

Corral your screens and devices

Just because you paired your new smart watch with your phone, it doesn't mean you have to accept the same set of notifications on it, so dig in and once again decide what you actually want there.

Are you actually going to read and reply to email and messages on your wrist? I'd respectfully suggest it won't happen very often, unless you are comfortable with dictating, or perhaps you have a massive phone and don't want to produce it every time. Everyone's life is different, and that's exactly why you need to control it. I have most alerts turned off on my wrist, except for good old-fashioned SMS messages, which these days tend to be application driven and often contain useful things like 2FA security codes.

If you're a real separator-type you might want a second phone for your work stuff anyway, and this can work well. Then you can leave it on your desk rather than your coffee table or bedside locker, and still enjoy your personal apps without work crossing into your personal time.

If that doesn't work for you, consider stuffing all your work apps on a back screen, or into a folder, so they are an additional tap away. Accessible if you need to check on something, but not grabbing your attention with their tempting red dopamine promises every time you pick up your phone to play Candy Crush.

Obviously, you need to manage the notification settings as well, and decide if you want silent alerts on a screen you'll see anyway, or if that will defeat the object. Just the difference between a screen-only alert, compared with anything that makes a noise or vibrates means you can control that particular flow simply by turning your phone face down.

Incidentally, if you enjoy reading non-work things like novels on an e-reader, I really recommend investing in a separate, dedicated device for that purpose, if you can justify the cost. For me, a non-backlit screen is far kinder to tired and burned-out eyes for reading in bed at the end of the day, and the lack of Twitter alerts running across the screen and zero ability to check on other things with a single tap, so that's well worth it..

Cultivate your attention and focus

It's a chilling but inevitable truth - the constant rush of likes and the endorsement they bring us, the flow of messages 24/7, and innate familiarity with how those notifications make us feel, is actually damaging our ability to use our minds consciously. To think, to concentrate, to decide where to put our attention for ourselves, instead of having it led exactly where a tech giant's head of marketing decides they want you to put it – therein lies your personal power. The evidence is in - big tech is measurably damaging our natural ability to use our brains.

The good news is, you can fight back, and if you want to have a successful career in any rapidly evolving knowledge-based industry I would argue that it's vital you do so. Our old friend Cal Newport called his best-seller 'Deep Work' for a reason, and he argues that it's crucial for competitive advantage and productivity to be able to concentrate for prolonged periods and create things. Back in 1990, long before we had a like button on anything, Mihaly Csikszentmihalyi taught us to aspire to 'flow,' that deep state of involvement in our present activity which nothing can distract from or penetrate our focus. In flow is where we reach incredible levels of creativity and involvement.

We'll look more closely at this in the next volume of Healthy Happy Homeworking when we explore productivity, but for now, be aware that mastery of this is a boundary issue. Every time you are distracted by an alert on your screen, you're giving away a little piece of your brain and your attention, which you can then no longer use for your original purpose, to something that probably doesn't deserve it.

Master your alerts, buy a dedicated Kindle,or even a book. A really intelligent friend recently told me she hadn't read the Wolf Hall trilogy, because she couldn't concentrate on that many pages, characters and plot complexity, even though she'd love to escape into it one day, perhaps on holiday. This woman has a PhD and manages an international team, who operate 24-7!

I don't have an easy answer to this, other than to suggest trying the following:

- Learn to meditate. It will help put you back in charge of deciding where your thoughts go, rather than your thoughts leading you. Because it's too easy for other influences to lead your thoughts too.

- Learn to be bored, to live without stimulus, for a while. Consciously avoid grabbing your phone when you have to wait in line for a few minutes, or during an ad break on TV.

- Practice concentrating on one input at a time. I am so guilty of cross-sensory multitasking - and while this can be efficient, it works against your ability to focus. Go for a walk with just your thoughts and no headphones one day. Listen to a podcast without playing a game on the screen at the same time

- Cultivate mindfulness, and keeping your attention in the present moment.

Monitoring and micromanagement

The other aspect of tech and your boundaries we need to talk about actually goes much deeper than the hardware and software involved.

What is your employer paying you for?

Do they own your time, from the point at which is it contractually available to them? Do they own your desktop? What do they value - the work you produce, or the hours you spend on it?

These abstract-sounding questions get to the heart of one way that technology can be used to erode trust and personal boundaries, in the work-from-home environment, not least because of the degree of data and analytics functionality embedded in modern collaboration tools. They say that what gets measured gets done, but does this mean that just because you can measure something, you should? Absolutely not.

Not long ago, Microsoft Office's 'Productivity Score' was highlighted by Austrian digital rights non-profit organisation Cracked Labs, for generating a rating of users based on aggregated data of their engagement right across the Office 365 tool suite. This can be used to provide managers with individual views on how many hours an employee has spent sending emails, using chat, the team channels they've posted to, and so on.

Microsoft pointed out in their defence that this feature was opt-in, designed to help IT admins provide technical support and guidance at an individual level, while also helping organisations make the most of their technology investments and collaboration practices. However, one of the problems is that nothing is 'opt-in' about it for the user, and the tool suite effectively normalises a highly intrusive level of worker surveillance.

This is bad enough in the office, but when such monitoring is used in a home-based setting - perhaps on devices also used for personal purposes - it becomes particularly icky and unpleasant. It's like school bullies who were once left in the playground following children home and into their personal space, often with devastating outcomes.

Microsoft's productivity tools are the least of it, compared with applications deliberately dedicated to employee surveillance, all of which have seen an explosion of use since the forced homeworking phenomena of the Coronavirus pandemic. Queries for "How to monitor employees working from home" increased by 1,705% in April and 652% in May 2020 compared with searches carried out the preceding year. Businesses like Time Doctor, Hubstaff, FlexiSPY and Activ Trak are doing very nicely out of the sheer lack of trust so many managers and organisations seem to have in the people working for them.

Many of these tools literally monitor down to the keystroke level. Typing on the slow side? Sorry, you can be penalised as inefficient. Or your manager might receive an alert if your keyboard is idle for a predetermined time. If this makes you so anxious your IBS flares up, you'd better take your laptop with you into the bathroom - just make sure your boss' spyware hasn't overridden your webcam settings first!

If you use email or messaging tools provided by your employer, you can reasonably expect they will have oversight over their appropriate use, and accept there's no such thing as a truly private conversation. If they provide you with a machine to work with, it's also reasonable for access to be blocked to certain websites or apps which are deemed too risky, and even if you are using your own machine, naturally there should be absolute control over corporate assets such as personal data and intellectual property.

But by and large, my feeling is that this kind of monitoring should be on an exceptional basis only. Configure your collaboration platform to detect breaches of compliance, like someone sending out an internal document Notify staff that personal communications may be archived or accessed if needed, then *leave them alone* unless there is a complaint or an issue of some description. When my teenage daughters first got smartphones and email, the deal was, I held the passwords and override access, and they knew I was really not interested in their messages to their friends and would only use that power if it became absolutely necessary.

Sure, I was paying for the phone and the contract, just as the employer is paying for your time when you're working for them, but that didn't mean trust had no place in establishing the norms of use. And unless you are cranking widgets on a production line, there has to be better ways of managing your actual work output than monitoring your keystrokes, or timing your use of each app. In the office, you might have felt great stress and personal pressure because of performance expectations driven by meaningful metrics like sales targets, KPIs, or key results areas, but at least they were based on a realistic proxy for the value you were providing within your role, as opposed to how many bashes your finger makes on a key.

On a more ongoing basis, there are many ways to make work and progress visible, to measure things which matter, and to drive desirable outcomes - like first call resolution rate in customer service, for example. You don't need to monitor every meaningless action someone takes, you need to be aware of the impact they're having, and how effective their work is.

Any organisation which finds itself resorting to this kind of intrusive employee surveillance, with total disregard for how this makes people feel *when they're in their own homes*, needs to take a good long look at their culture, their management training, and their levels of trust.

If this is happening where you work, you do have a choice - remember that when you can work from home, you can work for anyone.

CHAPTER 7: BOUNDARIES AND OTHER PEOPLE

One thing some people discovered for the first time during the Covid-related lockdowns is that working from home does not happen in a vacuum. Many of us actually got better at admitting and accepting the presence of others in our working days and spaces, through having no choice in the matter. - While I spent many of my early years in homeworking living with the expectation of hiding my home and family from detection at all times, this is hopefully one positive legacy of the whole pandemic experience.

Even if you live alone, there will always be other people around - in your community on and offline, and possibly sharing contention for your broadband infrastructure, if nothing else.

Working from home around children and family

My first experience of working from home happened when my eldest daughter was 6 months old. I hired a trainee nanny from a local college - they needed supervised placements for their students to gain experience, and I needed responsible care at the cheapest rate possible, so it was a good mutual deal. The fact that meeting the payment was still a big stretch for me was an amazing motivator when it came to being productive and focused.

I couldn't afford the nanny full-time, so I still had to work around the baby for part of the day, but those hours when somebody else had care of her in another room meant I could be working on phone calls or concentrating fully on the job, close at hand for feeds or dealing with questions or emergencies, but otherwise free to get my head down.

I learned early in my homeworking career the difference between working with and without a baby around, and I have eternal respect for all the boot-strapped entrepreneurs out there who get their stuff up and running between naps and nappies, and all the endless interruptions and distractions that life in the baby zone entails. It's an incredible achievement. I was lucky enough to have a salary to support me, so I didn't have to go down that path, or at least, not until my girls were old enough to master Netflix and their own iPads.

All the mummies who had no choice but to hand their little ones over to a carer and go back to someone else's office at the end of their maternity leave, you have my great respect. Whatever your motivations for so doing, I am sure that some days more than others, walking away from your baby each morning was harder than anything your working day brought. I vividly remember how much my mind was pulled away into the other room even when working from home - any change in routine, like teething or a fever, and it was almost impossible to close the door and leave it to someone else, even when I really had to. For those who weren't close at hand and had to delegate that decision making and care completely, I cannot begin to imagine the difficulties, however much your work was necessary for personal fulfilment, or small matters like putting food on the table. Mums - and Dads - are heroes.

Even though I regard myself as a highly integrated work-life blender as detailed above, when your children are little - and whenever they need you, at any age - it's impossible to not feel guilt, stress, and a need to compromise over and over, whenever work and family matters collide. You feel like you're short-changing one or other party at all times, because they both demand 100% attention, and I know this is no better for Mums in the office, dealing with calls from school or carers, trying to maintain that professional front, having coded phone conversations about agendas and deliverables with the childminder while fearful of judgement from all sides.

Of course, many aspects are easier when you work from home, and my impending new arrival was the main reason I made the shift in the first place. That doesn't mean the tension and the conflict disappear though, however idyllic it might sound to a reluctant new parent having to commute. The situation is perfectly summed up by a crystal clear and bittersweet memory from long ago: watching my toddler bashing self-importantly at her make-believe laptop on the coffee table, and imperiously advising her teddies that she couldn't play with them now because she was doing her emails!

So few parents - and by this I usually mean, few mothers - have a real choice about whether to work after having children. Either the costs of childcare mean it makes no sense for them to do so, or they cannot afford to lose the second income, regardless of the dent in it, without serious lifestyle compromises which will affect their child's future life in the long term.

The best I could do at the time was pay someone else to be there for her, and later her sister, for the hours I needed to be focused on earning a living. And at least when you work from home you do have some flexibility regarding the professional status of that carer. As well as the trainee nannies, we had au pairs from various nations, which is a very affordable solution and well worth considering, provided you have space to accommodate a long-term guest in a home which already has an office crammed into it somewhere.

It's good advance practice for later dealing with hormonal teenagers, but even though we found some wonderful people who remain friends to this day, it's important to realise that au pairs are usually completely untrained, and won't usually bring any formal work experience in caring for children or babies to the table. They should never be in sole charge of an infant. As such, if you pursue this path, that boundary will always remain more porous.

We chose all the applicants carefully, following up all the references, even though that meant duplicating the work of the agency, and grappling with early online translation tools, because we were entrusting our children and our home to a stranger from far away. Perhaps we were lucky, but almost of the time this setup worked very well for us, creating the flexibility I needed to grow a business, and bringing interesting cultural and linguistic experiences into our home. Whenever we employed a new girl, she would at first accompany me to the door of meetings, and walk around outside with the buggy, so they were never more than a few minutes away. As my trust and their experience developed, things reached a point where I felt confident enough to leave them at home while I took the train into the city.

Until this trust develops with any child carer, you don't really have any type of boundary in place anyway, because your heart and mind is always elsewhere. You need to really work at finding the right people and organisations to fit into your life, and also your kids' lives as they get older. This includes nurseries and schools. They must feel okay to you, because otherwise you won't be able to let go of worry and focus on work - or at least, I couldn't.

Domestic matters, childcare, and your working relationships

Because of this, once I got to the point of hiring people to work for me from home, I insisted they had adequate childcare in place, at least for younger kids, anyway. This takes you into murky waters from an HR and employment law point of view incidentally, so you need to take care to address this question with ALL candidates regardless of age, gender, and so on. This delicate issue is best approached via a conversation about being able to provide accommodation for home-based working that's free from interruption and distraction under normal circumstances.

Of course, circumstances vary, and part of working from home is being able to have greater flexibility for inset days, childhood fevers, and so on. And for fun stuff like school sports events and performances, it's generally much easier for a home-based worker to pop out for short periods to show up as a parent. No one ever missed things like this on my watch.

Keeping boundaries clear here can become more difficult though, and a lot will depend on the prevailing culture and practice in your workplace, if you are employed.

If you're fortunate enough to work somewhere where your effectiveness is judged by what you produce and create, as opposed to the time you show logged in to a piece of software or appearing to be present in a messaging app, you can sort things out with good time management and personal integrity. On days when personal stuff makes demands on you during normal work time, you will work around it, and get things done either faster or later.

If you are accountable to a manager or work system that mandates a higher degree of presenteeism and time logged on, you need to negotiate those boundaries, transparently and proactively. It's difficult for anyone to object if you can explain that you're taking your kid to a dental appointment at midday, so you logged on 2 hours early to get X finished in good time.

I have known people who were never comfortable having to explain in detail about appointments relating to their children, but so much depends on your relationship with your manager, and with the rest of your team.

At one time, I worked in a situation where I was the only home-based worker and one of very few parents, certainly the only one with a baby. The corporate message was loud and clear: Don't ask don't tell, get your work done and delivered, and you can have as much flexibility as you want, just don't bore us with the messy details. Once I had a colleague with a new-born, however, a different culture emerged in our own team, and we shared and supported each other around the domestic things as much as around the work things. We were all on top of each others' kid's Christmas shows and vaccination schedules, and no one would have dreamed of saying they were 'Just popping out' without sharing why. That stuff went in the office calendar first, and client work fitted around it.

At least in both these situations there was no case of covering up or dissembling, in counterpoint to a vivid childhood memory of my own. I recall lying in my parent's bed with a high fever, and being startled to hear my own mother *lying through her teeth* to her boss, about becoming suddenly unwell herself. Back then, there was no acceptable way to explain that her child was sick and couldn't go to school, so she needed a day off at short notice.

Of course, that was decades ago, and a time when working from home would have been a technological impossibility, as well as a time when fewer mothers worked outside the home anyway. It would hopefully be less of an occurrence today, but I've often thought of that memory when considering the kind of team culture I want to create in my own enterprises. It's about honesty and integrity in your conversations and commitments to each other, as well as the psychological safety to bring your whole self to work, and I certainly hope it's easier now than it was back in the 1980s.

As a manager, if someone on my team has a sick child, I want to know about it. Then I can support them personally and help them navigate any temporary changes in their availability, concentration, and judgement as a result. If they need to take personal time off at short notice, it's best if the whole team can understand the situation. Ideally there is some degree of personal trust equity established in all the working relationships in the team so everyone has everyone's back, and will support each other individually when it's needed. We all have personal things going on which affect our ability to do our best work, and this is certainly not territory exclusive to new parents. I'd much rather work in an environment where people feel safe to bring their personal issues to the table in a balanced and reasonable way, while offering equal consideration to their colleagues when necessary.

When you work closely as a team like this, you can support each other within the workplace - virtual or physical - and maintain a united front in so far as external communications are concerned. Back before working from home was common, there would be different ways of handling similar messages. My team knew I was watching my youngest child's stage debut as Mary, complete with tea towel headdress and favourite baby doll, and they were eagerly looking forward to the photos I'd share later. However, they would simply inform clients I was occupied in a meeting until after lunch, and my out-of-office email message told the same story.

Indeed, back in the day when I ran a research fieldwork agency from home, we often had a good chuckle internally, wondering what our clients would say if they could actually see us, where and how we got their projects managed. We were lucky enough to work with some big global brands with high professional standards, and if I put on a suit to go and visit their very impressive offices, I couldn't help but imagine their faces if they were to see the garden shed I worked in. While we didn't lie about the fact that we all worked from home, it wasn't something I would go out of my way to share early in the business relationship, nor to paint too detailed a picture of exactly how and where their work got done. It's far better to stay focused on results.

Later, as a freelancer, the same thing applied, and like everyone else, I take advantage of the anonymity and flexibility of remote work life when I have to.

I remember once blatantly lying to a tech founder I had finally secured a hard-fought interview with, only to be confronted with an urgent domestic situation. Postponement wasn't an option, so I told him my webcam wasn't working, sorry, and we would have to do the interview 'audio only.' I had no intention of sharing that I was sitting in the garden in my bra, drenched in nit lotion, combing through the seething head of the child sitting on the floor in front of me.

No one can multi-task like a home-working mother. And yes, I did triple-check that my webcam was deactivated.

Children and your home office

Of course, this boundary works both ways.

I have worked from home since my eldest was 6 months old, and it's always been part of her life. Mummy goes to this particular room in the house for hours at a time, and we're really not supposed to bother her while she's in there.

Except it's Mummy, and it's home, and she's just through there - and this is really difficult for little ones to understand. Sometimes only Mummy will do, and the sternest/loveliest au pair in the world can't keep them from seeking you out, when everyone realises that this grazed knee is best kissed better by the person they want. So you have to be ready to shift gears fast.

As they get older, their requirements change, but they still need you. For help with homework, for the pressing issues of co-ordinating lifts and play dates, or just for listening to vital topics regarding friends and boyfriends/girlfriends, skincare and fashion. Then there are those moments when a letter from school, which has languished in a book bag for a fortnight, has to have a signature on it right NOW, otherwise they're going to miss the trip.

Kids of homeworking parents always have beautifully presented school projects. They learn early on to reboot a router, to wrestle a printer with a paper jam, and hopefully to return all charging cables they 'borrow' to the correct drawer after use. Their parents go through suspicious quantities of consumables like post-it notes and highlighters if they're on an expense account, as well as mobile streaming data. It can be frustrating when you find out your eldest has offered to print out lengthy group presentations and visuals, because - as they report in hushed, incredulous tones - *Marta's parents haven't even got an office at home.*

They also see their parents working, which is something I think is often overlooked in importance. When I was a child, both my parents at various times went to work in offices, but I was never sure exactly what that involved. There were important pieces of paper which accompanied them back and forth, as well as special clothes, but the work itself? I had no idea, and on the rare occasions we visited them there, it all appeared rather fun and centred around tea and biscuits.

While my girls have certainly, on occasion, lost out on my attention due to demands of work, they can at least see that work close-up, and have done so from an early age, thereby making the connection between effort and reward. They see that work absorbs time, attention and sometimes emotion. They witness bad days, and also good days. They see it's tough when a sudden surge of work lands on me as a freelancer, and we all have to miss out on doing something together to meet a new deadline, but they enjoy the family day out that the gig pays for during the following month.

I think it's important for our kids to see us reading, writing, listening, and concentrating, and also experiencing delayed gratification. If I am going to take tomorrow afternoon off to see you in the sports tournament, then this evening I have to get this piece of work done - so you can make dinner.

While there are some aspects of work life which require 100% of your attention, or even total silence, you should never feel compelled to hide your professional commitments from your children, or to protect them from the realities of working for a living. They'll have to do that themselves someday. There is, sadly and inevitably, a correlation between children whose parents do not work, growing up to experience a similar lifestyle themselves; this is far from coincidental. And the little girl who told her teddies she was too busy to play with them because of doing her emails will probably earn a living bashing a keyboard herself at some point, which will require compromise from her dependents too.

For this reason, I work with the door open whenever I can, literally and metaphorically. That's easy enough now my girls are older, and understand the idea that when I am at my desk in my office, I am generally working, and by default I should be left undisturbed. But if they're passing and want a chat, or want to print something, or bring me a coffee, well that's just fine. It's what an open door might signal in a shared office. At other times, I'll close the door because I am having a meeting, and it's better if there's minimal background noise and disturbance.

This is a moving target however, and these norms and expectations have evolved as my girls have grown older, and as the world has grown into home working. I have some clients who have crossed over into the status of friends anyway, and will always say hi to the girls or my husband if a cuppa arrives mid-meeting, and the same can happen on both sides. Although it WAS surprising once, when the husband of an associate wandered into shot wearing just a pair of Speedos, but at least he had something on, I guess.

Even before the remote revolution of 2020, the trend to embrace the realities of working from home being in a context rather than a vacuum was on its way. In 2017, Robert Kelly, associate professor of Political Science at Pusan National University in South Korea, became a viral sensation while being interviewed live on a rolling news show. If you haven't seen it, or need to revisit, Google "BBC Dad." Watch his delightful 4-year-old daughter stroll confidently into the room like a total boss, followed by her little brother in a baby walker, and his mortified wife, scrambling to retrieve them both, while hilariously failing to remain below the camera's angle of view.

Meanwhile, Professor Kelly remains rigidly composed, desperately trying to continue with his serious political commentary while pretending nothing untoward is happening.

The family became a social media sensation as a result, and it appears to have done nothing but good for Kelly's public speaking career. The clip and its stars gained renewed attention in 2020, when suddenly everyone was working from home, and the situation's resonance gained vast new audience and understanding.

Indeed, I sincerely hope that this erosion of the erstwhile rigid boundaries between children and work is one positive legacy of the Covid lockdowns. On more than one occasion throughout 2020, we saw TV news broadcasts and other live media interrupted by additional cast members, and while the Kelly family incident would have been uproariously amusing at any time and place, today it's just one more example of kids busting in to work where they are neither expected nor invited.

For my work interviewing lots of tech folks, their end of the call previously tended to be conducted from some groovy downtown co-working space, prior to spring 2020. Once everyone was based at home and frequently home-schooling at the same time, it was a great leveller, and indeed it could be really positive. As a journalist, it can be difficult to create connection in a brief call, and encourage people to talk sincerely and spontaneously about something that isn't in the official press release. Frankly, if a pre-schooler crawls onto their lap and joins in for a while, it breaks the ice. They might be talking about a huge Series A funding round, then have to pause to help open a carton of juice, and express their human side. I hate to generalise, but Dads are generally more inclined to be embarrassed and apologetic about this interruption, while Mums just scoop the little one up and continue the conversation without missing a beat. I usually record interviews, not being old-school enough to have learned shorthand, so I always explain that I'll delete the video as soon as I have written it up. Often the call continues with the additional participant staying, and sometimes sharing their own professional accomplishments by way of Lego or artwork, even if these never make it to my finished editorial.

Of course, there are other conversations where you absolutely must not be interrupted. It's a professional discourtesy and/or breach of confidence to be dealing with HR or disciplinary matters while some little person is waving crayons about. These are situations you need to schedule with the support of other members of the household or paid childcare, when you can.

Other times, if I am recording a podcast or video interview, I have notices on the door, reinforced by WhatsApp messages sent before logging out that I REALLY don't want to be disturbed. This includes music or door banging, due to the weird acoustics in our house. I am also in negotiations with the family to get the printer out of my office. Not only do other people suddenly decide they need hard copies of homework documents at the strangest times, but the senile old machine has also developed a habit of performing loud maintenance on itself at unexpected moments. Unfortunately, I cannot do anything about the neighbours who seem to have a sixth sense for the most annoying moment to fire up their home and garden power tools whenever I hit the record button.

My aforementioned friend with younger children who worked with them to create a series of different notices for her office door, designed this to be understood even by the youngest one, when they were in the early days of lockdown home education. She wanted them to feel free to come to her when they needed to, which was nearly all the time, but she also needed to safeguard her privacy to work with colleagues intensely when necessary. This included providing emotional support in challenging circumstances, and holding the space safely and peacefully was essential. So she and the kids created signs which conveyed colour-coded scales of interruption that nobody could misunderstand, which the older siblings could reinforce with the toddler.

The final point about working from home around your kids will come as no surprise to any parent: it's a moving target.

Those boundaries you think you have nailed will always be dynamic, because the kids change, the work changes, or a new situation arises. As a parent, you've known about this since the earliest days of trying to establish routines of feeding and sleep, and it will continue to evolve as long as you share space with those most fascinating, complex, and maddening little people - we wouldn't have it any other way, right? Life will be much less stressful if you accept that, just when you think you've got it all worked out, that's the precise moment something will shift.

Working from home within your community

Educating your kids around expectations and behaviour when you're working from home is one thing, but often they're not the only ones who impinge on your boundaries.

They have friends, for a start, which is manageable when they are little and a bit scared of you, but then they get older and the sleepovers start, along with the influence on YOUR kids to take behavioural liberties in the presence of their peers. For a long time, my other half shared his office with what also passes for a spare bedroom in our house, and simply getting overnight guests of the teenage variety up and out of it in time to do a day's work was frequently a challenge, never mind restoring the space itself to some kind of habitability.

But long before the kids are arranging their own social lives, you deal with the conspiracy of other parents, particularly those who are frantically juggling working outside the home on a daily basis. Sometimes they don't appreciate that you have professional commitments, just the same as they do.

I have nothing but respect for anyone who manages to juggle actually going to work and childcare, and I know such arrangements are frequently very complex, relying on a huge range of factors to come together and stay that way, with multiple interlocking parts. As such, it only takes one of these elements to unravel - a car won't start, the school goes on strike, or a childminder is unwell - and it all falls apart. That's when the parents occasionally develop stress induced retrospective hearing defects, and decide that when you said 'I work from home', you actually meant 'I operate a free daycare resource from my house at zero minutes notice.' *So then, is it OK if I just drop Ella round to you/ can you collect her when you pick yours up at lunchtime?*

Bitter? No not really, and what are friends for but to help out at times of need. Sometimes it's OK, and sometimes it's a huge inconvenience. Looking back, I can see that there were definitely times when things got a little unbalanced on the fair and reasonable front, but every relationship has different boundaries and expectations. I would only advise in this situation to not be a doormat - no-one is keeping score, but it shouldn't all be one-sided. You'll need a favour one day, so be sure to ask for it.

By the way, if your au pair is suddenly taking care of two extra charges, they should be tipped - by your buddy, not by you - for babysitting. This is a bonus on top of your mutual working arrangement.

In terms of give and take, you *are* at home anyway, and as such it could be a fairly painless way to help out. As soon as your kids are old enough to play with minimal supervision, they might interrupt less when there are two of them around. It's fun for your child, provided they are genuinely friends and not circumstantial children-of-your-friends which can be much less fun to be stuck with, and it provides them with the company of others when they can't have yours because of your work commitments.

For me, it only tended to cross the line when it came with expectations that ate into my precious work time, and that was generally due to thoughtlessness or forgetfulness. Sure, she is welcome to come back here after school and have tea, but I won't be able to drive her to football practice after that *because I'll be working*, so you'll need to arrange for someone else to pick her up from ours.

At some point, you may look back fondly on those days you were asked first, as in a street where everyone commutes, the only person around during the day can end up playing a pivotal role in the community by default.

Again, you need to apply a test of reasonableness, and dig your heels in, especially when mission-creep is occurring. Agree with your neighbour it's OK to give your address for the delivery of a package which will need a signature - you're at home anyway. But they have to appreciate that the doorbell will interrupt your work. We will dig into this more in the next book, but the actual cost to your productivity is far more than the 2 minutes of answering the door, because the interruption breaks your creative flow. So it may be alright when their emergency passport is delivered, but it's not OK to expect you to take in their online shopping every week. That's not fair.

Similarly if they have someone coming round to service the washing machine or something, they might say, *"You work on a laptop don't you? You could even bring it around."* Well, yes you could, and if it's a good friend in a fix, then you probably will, but you need to let them know that it's not ideal, and you'll get less work done than you would at your desk, where you have all your stuff and your personalised setup.

Difficulties can arise when it's not your dear friends and neighbours who are the ones taking the mickey, but the postal workers and couriers themselves, who soon catch on to the fact that yes, you're always home. Just sitting next to the doorbell, awaiting their pleasure, and glad to act as a parcel depot for half the neighbourhood.

This is really tricky, because it's not your friend's fault, but maybe they can help you out. Explain you're on a deadline, or busy with calls most mornings. If they have Amazon stuff coming, please could they amend the delivery instructions to leave the order by their gate instead of bringing it round to you? Tell them you probably won't be able to answer the door, so you'd hate for them to take it away again.

You could even invest in one of those doorbells which comes with a video entry phone and/or runs off an app on your phone. If you can see it's the courier who knows you by name YET again, but you are not expecting any deliveries yourself, then you won't need to apologise to the person you're in a meeting with and go charging down the stairs for the third time today,

In some ways, it's even harder when you freelance or work a flexible schedule, because you are manifestly, well - *flexible*. If you can buy your groceries when it's quieter mid-afternoon, can you pick up theirs as well? Can I just ask you about this thing, while you're passing? You can write the script to suit.

It's up to you set boundaries - with your friends, with your lonely elderly neighbour, with your relative who calls for a chat after lunch. Nobody else will carve out those edges for you, and it can be genuinely hard. You might need some practice. Try any, or all, of these examples for starters.

"I am just in the middle of something, can I get back to you?"

Yes, I did pick up the phone, because you're my friend and I love you. But if it's just for a chat, then we need to do this another time, because *I'm working right now*.

You can use this with colleagues, family, even clients/managers - who should respect you for respecting your own time and attention. It's essentially a prompt triage, which encourages them to immediately state their case and urgency, so you can prioritise on the fly. If there's an emergency you can deal with it, but if they want a chat you can explain you'll ring them back as soon as you're done for the day.

"I'll need to check my diary and get back to you."

This is a good one, because it buys you time, if you struggle with that handy yet complete sentence, "No". If you possibly can, be assertive and transparent and decline straightaway. But if you have any doubts, or if you're worried you're going to start wobbling and over-justifying, then blame the schedule, to which you are just as much in thrall as everyone else. Then send the negative response by email as soon as possible.

This tactic helps reinforce the idea that you HAVE a schedule, you know-commitments. It's a double winner, buying you time to think things over before you get co-opted, and subtly let people know you have other things to do. Work things, life things - not their business.

"I have a deadline"

On behalf of all journalists I willingly donate this phrase for general use. We all have deadlines - time-limited commitments to others, AND to ourselves.

If you've carved out the rest of the morning to catch up on your admin, that's a pre-existing commitment, to a very important stakeholder. You can smile and hurry past the lovely retired neighbour, and have no obligation to stop for a chat, if it's in the middle of your work day.

Back to school... And the blurred line

A final point on community boundaries, specifically for parents of school aged children. I am probably speaking mostly to mothers here, based on the assumptions I have met in the minds of others.

I hope this will be less of an issue post-pandemic, going forward, but back when my girls were in primary school, there were two distinct tribes of mums involved. Those who worked outside the home, and those who did not. While they might have shared a WhatsApp group, they could not have been more distinct from one another, in their lifestyles and their patterns of behaviour. The former didn't show up much on WhatsApp anyway, reflecting their fleeting appearances, dropping off at the school gate early as they whisked off to the metro station.

The full time Mums, on the other hand, had time to stop and chat, and to do all the other things - plan collections for joint birthday gifts, make costumes for the Christmas show, carpool to basketball, and volunteer for endless school activities. I know full well these things would not have happened without their willing involvement, and their willingness to hold endless meetings about these issues in local coffee shops.

I was always neither fish nor fowl. Doing the school run in jeans and stopping to say hi - but swerving the sports shuttles and fundraising committees, and really not able to go for coffee this morning, sorry. *"I'd need to check my schedule."*

It was difficult at times, because no one knew quite what box to put me in. *Well, obviously we didn't ask Elena even though it's really her turn, because SHE WORKS...* Hello, yes, so do I! Because you see me at every class assembly and concert, it looks like I am having the best of both worlds. Able to make it to all the fun stuff, the things I really want to do, but avoiding the genuinely hard work which goes into making any community function, which schools increasingly seem to rely on, even to make the delivery of education happen.

Hands up, yes, I did have the best of both worlds - and I was proud of it. I probably didn't earn as much as the commuter Mums dashing off to catch the train, but I never missed the things that mattered to me at school, because I was based nearby, and I had flexibility over my schedule. I was keenly aware that I never did playground volunteer duty or classroom support, but I showed up during English Week and things like that - I just couldn't do it all. If I had, I would have been letting down my colleagues and clients, but most of all, myself and my high standards of delivery.

Does any parent ever let go of the guilt? Please get in touch and let me know.

What I hope for in the future is that there will be less of a them-and-us dichotomy, less of a split between working and non-working parents. I have never met a parent who doesn't work extremely hard, and whether or not that comes with a salary attached really shouldn't matter.

We all have an inalienable right to set boundaries around our work and our personal time.

CHAPTER 8: SUSTAINABLE AND DYNAMIC BOUNDARIES

I realise the inevitable conclusion to this question of boundaries when you work from home, is that there are no firm answers to be had.

Everything is flexible, fluid, and continually changing - but I urge you to acknowledge this quality, and work with it. Ignore the 'rules' according to anyone else, because it's your home, your work, your mind, your family, your career, and your community. Get your individual red lines clear, and communicate them when and how you need to, with whoever needs to know.

It's not always easy in practice, and this is one of the hardest aspects of working from home to truly get a grip on - although there's a subtle yet hugely effective benefit when you do so. Those moments when you feel like you have it all in balance, remember to bask in that feeling and enjoy it. Because, you guessed it, it's bound to come crashing down again soon.

To assist you further, we have lots of support to offer you, over in our friendly community at https://facebook.com/groups/healthyhappyhomeworking.

You can also follow us on Twitter @hhhomeworking and Instagram @healthyhappyhomeworking, and sign up for email alerts of book and content releases at healthyhappyhomeworking.com - including advance notice of special pricing and new products, on an occasional basis.

The next book in the series, for publication late 2021, will explore the ways we remain productive and effective, managing our time and motivation while homeworking. So expect lots of discussion and debate about that in our community, and we'd love to include your thoughts and ideas.

Tell me what you need to know, what you want to read about and learn about, to make your work from home better - and I'll do my very best to deliver.

ACKNOWLEDGEMENTS

As I hope this book has made clear, working from home does not happen in a vacuum, not even the solitary process of writing a book.

In addition to the family and friends who have supported and encouraged me along the way, I wanted to express my thanks in particular to all the members of the Healthy Happy Homeworking community - and I use that term very loosely to embrace not only the 'official' Facebook group, but all of those who have responded to broader questions and conversations on Twitter and elsewhere, and my coaching and consulting clients.

You'll see some of their direct contributions woven through the text, and that's one reason this book is slightly longer than the previous volume. I really needed that input, particularly from those readers who might not have chosen to work from home in the first place, and whose experiences through the challenges of 2020 were not always positive (you know who you are, and your generous sharing will help others get things right from the start).

Early readers of this book, including Tanya and Rowena, gave me invaluable detailed feedback, in particular from the employee perspective, one in which my experience was decades out of date. Even a short book is better for wider input.

As well as writing me a lovely foreward, Rowena was a huge personal support to me through a difficult year, when so much more than writing books was going on - proving once and for all, where any proof needed, that distance is no object to being there for someone and looking after them emotionally. Pilar,

Niamh, and lots of other lovely friends also had my back at this time in ways I will never forget, and my family in the UK - who I haven't been able to see physically for far too long, but feel closer to than ever after what we have all been through together in recent months.

Anyway, back to the book!

Sandra's professional and timely editing tightened everything up where I was inclined to ramble, and sharpened the prose for better impact, particularly important when a book is written over a prolonged period of time – I am so grateful for this support. And my 'Millennium baby' Cass who told her teddies she was too busy to play because of her emails, has now grown up into a very competent proof reader.

And on the broader community front, I'd like to personally thank everyone who took the time to review and rate volume one, "Out Of The Office". For independent authors it is a huge challenge to break through to new audiences and spread the word, and every bit of feedback and social proof matters, so it makes such a difference.

And however much the number and ratings matter in practical terms, there really is nothing like the personal satisfaction and joy, when you know your words have connected with and helped someone you will never meet. While it's really very easy, honestly, I know it takes time and intention to go back to the site you bought from and bother to share your thoughts - so I know I speak for every author or other creative professional in the world, when I express my huge gratitude, for everyone taking the time to do so.

FURTHER READING AND RESEARCH

This was never intended to be a textbook or academic work of reference, but in addition to the table of contents, you may find the following links useful:

Chapter 3:
Brain.FM: You can check this out free for a month at brain.fm/invite/G9029PV2pK if you're curious, to see if it help you.

Chapter 4
Integrators and separators - you can read the original paper here: https://hbr.org/2020/07/building-work-life-boundaries-in-the-wfh-era.

Thinking Remote: Inspiration For Leaders Of Distributed Teams (2019), I co-authored with Pilar Orti. Find it at https://geni.us/HHHThinkingRemote and all good bookstores…

Chapter 5
Research about reflection to consolidate learning http://k12accountability.org/resources/For-Principals/Learning_Through_Reflection.pdf

Also, do take a look at Hal Elrod's Miracle Morning, and all the Cal Newport books mentioned.

Chapter 6

Here's more about the Cracked Labs exposure of Microsoft Office's 'productivity score', and the changes which resulted: https://digit.fyi/microsoft-office-365-tracking-features-attacked-as-surveillance/

Chapter 7

That famous 'BBC Dad' interview - go on, you know you want to see it again: https://www.bbc.com/news/av/world-39232538

ABOUT THE AUTHOR

Following an early career in community development and voluntary sector training and facilitation in her native London, Maya transitioned to full-time home-based working at the turn of the millennium, founding a market research fieldwork agency. She taught herself to develop and manage what turned out to be a fully remote team, in an era when this was still rare — and when the technology infrastructure was prehistoric, compared to present day.

As her team grew and practices evolved, she relocated to the Spanish Costa Blanca, in pursuit of a healthier and happier lifestyle for her young family. She ended up writing a tech and social media column for the local English newspaper, and has been freelancing full-time since 2017 — as an author, journalist and podcaster, now settled in Valencia on the Eastern coast of Spain.

In 2018 she became an e-resident of Estonia, and since then, trades as BlockSparks OÜ, telling the stories of the social impact of technology and future trends. She writes about subjects ranging from collaboration platforms to cryptocurrency, and writes and podcasts regularly for London-based remote work consultancy Virtual Not Distant, as well as writing for UC Today, and a range of other publications. She has written a novel about bitcoin, Beyond The Chain, and also co-authored Thinking Remote: Inspiration for Leaders of Distributed Teams.

Despite her passion for technology, Maya is also a big fan of unplugging from all of it from time to time and immersing herself in the joys of live music, travel, hiking, culture, yoga, and all that her chosen Spanish home has to offer. So, if she's not at her desk you'll find her on the beach or up a mountain, where all her best creative ideas seem to come her way.

www.ingramcontent.com/pod-product-compliance
Lightning Source LLC
Chambersburg PA
CBHW070604220526
45467CB00003B/1286